You Can't AFFORD to Break Up

How an Empty Wallet and a Dirty Mind Can Save Your Relationship

Stacey Nelkin
and
Paul Schienberg, Ph.D.

iUniverse, Inc.
New York   Bloomington

You Can't AFFORD to Break Up
How an Empty Wallet and a Dirty Mind
Can Save Your Relationship

iUniverse books may be ordered through booksellers or by contacting:

iUniverse
1663 Liberty Drive
Bloomington, IN 47403
www.iuniverse.com
1-800-Authors (1-800-288-4677)

Because of the dynamic nature of the Internet, any Web addresses or links contained in this book may have changed since publication and may no longer be valid.

ISBN: 978-1-4401-8129-0 (sc)
ISBN: 978-1-4401-8128-3 (ebk)

Library of Congress Control Number: 2009910870

Printed in the United States of America

iUniverse rev. date: 12/10/2009

For Marco, my best friend and husband, whose inspiration and encouragement made this all happen—and to Antonia, Noah, and Stella. —Stacey Nelkin

To the memory of my father, whose energy, trust, and honesty gives me courage to execute my dreams; to my mother, who gave me life and saved it many times; and to my brother, whose constant love is an anchor. —Paul Schienberg

Contents

Acknowledgments

Stacey Nelkin:

This book simply would not exist without the incredible talent and intelligence of Liel Leibovitz. Thank you!

Robert Astle, thank you for your belief in us.

And thank you to Marco Greenberg—for not only your love and support, but because you were the one to introduce us all to each other!

Paul Schienberg:

I want to thank my patients over the past thirty-five years who have given me the opportunity to travel down the "yellow brick road" with them and rediscover the essence of their unique natures and apply them to their lives.

Great appreciation goes to the members of my Men's Support Group (Fred, Bob, David, Gil, Bud, and Edward). We have met once a month for more than fourteen years. They have shared with me the complex wonders of being a man and given me the psychological space and caring to discover my ability to love.

Thanks must go to Liel Leibovitz who has offered his creative energy and talents to bring the book to an amazing completion. Without his enthusiasm for the project, we would not have been able to share our ideas with clarity and freshness.

Robert Astle provided direction and insight. He has helped us see the relevance of this book to our culture and economic times. He joined us on our mission, always acted selflessly, and believed in this project and in us.

You Can't Afford to Ignore This Book

In so many ways, these are the worst of times: banks are collapsing, insurance companies are crashing down, and mortgages are spiraling out of control. Call us crazy, but we believe that these are also the best of times: with no cash to spare and no disposable income to distract us, now is the perfect time to forget about our stock portfolio and instead take stock of our relationships with our partners. Whether you're married or not, whether you've been together for five decades or five months, whether you and your partner live together or apart, the chances are that you bicker from time to time, occasionally want to strangle one another, and, on a few dark occasions, also contemplate breaking up. Hey, we all do. It's perfectly normal. However, the good news is that—as the title of this book suggests—you can't afford to break up.

We don't mean just in the economic sense, although, frankly, who can afford divorce lawyers nowadays? No, we're talking about something much deeper. Call it the first principle of emotional economics: until you figure out who you are and what you want, until you find a way to communicate with your partner honestly and openly, until you both learn to treat your relationship as a blank canvas on which you two can paint your lives together as you'd like to live, you're never going to make things work. Instead, you'll be investing immense amounts of energy in failed relationship after failed relationship, throwing away money and time, and wondering why you can't catch a break. And that, we're sure you'll agree, is just wasteful. We're here to give you the tools to avoid these mistakes—now and in the future.

Why are we qualified? Because one of us is a renowned therapist and the other a celebrated actress, and by now you probably know enough about relationships to know how much of it is psychology and how much theatre. Together, we'll tell you everything you need to know about how to talk and listen better, how to act up and spice up your love life, and how to come to terms with wild and untamed things such as your sexuality.

We'll also be talking about money—who isn't, nowadays?—and trying to convince you to see it as what it is, namely a sexy and thrilling source for fun and adventure rather than the source of all your anxieties and woes. When it comes to cash, it's not about whether you have it or not, but how you think about it and what you do with it that matters.

Ready to jumpstart your sex life, save your relationship, and save money? Read on.

Five Romantic Things to Do Under $5

Nothing's better than bubbles. Get naked and hop in the bath together.

Forget wine: beer is cheaper, and it'll take you back to the good ol' lustful days of high school.

Skip that meal and spend your cash on chocolate instead: buy two truffles, feed each other, and indulge.

Most museums will let you pay what you wish at least one evening per week. Go. Art is hot. Ever noticed all those naked people in paintings?

Get a bus ticket to some lovely bit of nature outside of town, lie on the grass, and make out. Nature can make you very randy.

Introduction

Amy and Dan met in graduate school, married the week after graduation, and had their first child right away. Two years later, when their second daughter was born, they were finally ready to pack in their fun, carefree life in the city and move to a nearby suburb. They searched for a bigger house, a better school district, and a more kid-friendly atmosphere. As they shoved the last boxes into the packed U-Haul and drove toward their new home and their new life, they shared sentimental stories about their time as a young couple. They talked about the bars that they used to hang out in until the wee hours of the morning, the theatre tickets they spent every disposable dollar buying, and the ski trips to Vermont with friends. These were fun times, they agreed, but the times ahead looked even better: a family of their own, a place to grow old together, and building a life. It was what they'd always wanted.

The suburbs, they soon learned, were nothing like the soul-crushing, numbingly boring wilderness that movies and television shows often portray them as. In fact, Dan and Amy loved everything about their new neighborhood: the people seemed genuinely friendly and many were in precisely the same spot in life—young couples adjusting to parenthood and moving up in their careers. Although evening outings would end earlier—there were kids to put to bed and babysitters to relieve—they found that social life away from the city was just as robust. They loved the space they suddenly had—especially after years of living in a shoebox of an apartment! Amy loved having a garden and planted tomatoes and radishes in the back yard. Dan turned the huge basement into the rec room of his dreams, buying a few used video game machines online and building his own personal arcade. Each of the girls had her own room, and the kitchen was large enough to allow both Amy and Dan, both amateur cooks, to experiment with roasts and stews and cakes.

Slowly, however, their relationship—once warm and loving and energetic—began to wilt. Neither of them could explain it, but they both felt it happening. With demanding jobs and young kids and dozens of social obligations every week, all they usually wanted to do when they were finally in their bedroom was put on the comfiest pair of pajamas, snuggle under the blanket, and sleep for as long as their schedules would let them. Sex, once a daily activity, gradually decreased to a few times per month. They also fought more than they used to—nothing serious, but the small, silly arguments were just enough to make things more difficult. Talking to his therapist one morning, Dan said he was afraid that the magic was beginning to fade from their relationship.

The economy didn't help things much. Neither Dan nor Amy was a financial genius, but they weren't irresponsible, either. They did everything they were told to do—they invested in diversified funds, had some savings, retirement plans, and a sensible mortgage. When the company that handled their finances went belly up, their 401(k)s were basically worthless, and they suddenly found themselves thinking about every penny they spent. They once took two vacations per year; now, one had to suffice. They once indulged in buying each other nice gifts for their birthdays, which were two weeks apart; now, they set a $100 limit per gift. They once took the girls out to a nice restaurant at least twice per month; now, they drove to the discount store and bought in bulk to save money.

This new, tight lifestyle did very little to help things get more romantic. Their fights became more frequent—and more ferocious. Worrying about money added a lot of anxiety to an already stressful relationship. Talking to his mother one day, Dan admitted that if things weren't so tight, he would probably leave Amy.

*   *   *

Megan and Tony had it all. They were in their late thirties and both had spent their entire lives obsessing over their careers—they both had much to show for it. A financial whiz kid who put himself through Princeton working odd jobs and investing his modest salary in the stock market, Tony made his first million before he turned thirty-five. Working as a senior executive in a major investment bank, his yearly bonus alone was enough to buy large houses, fast cars, and expensive vacations. Tony couldn't imagine life without summers in the Hamptons, without winters in Aspen, without dining daily in Manhattan's most exclusive restaurants.

The night he met Megan, at a black-tie gala at the Metropolitan Museum of Art, he called up his best friend and said he'd just met the woman he wanted to marry. Megan, he thought, was a female version of him: she was a hard-working and extremely successful designer. She was not shy about flaunting her wealth or power—and she flaunted it all right. Fifteen minutes into their first conversation, Tony already knew that purse she was carrying was a Birkin—the Hermes creation that's considered the holy grail of leather goods—that her necklace came from Tiffany's, and that she was on her way to a weekend in Venice the following morning, just because she felt like it. Tony loved Megan's confidence and swagger; he made sure to ask for her phone number. A year later, they got married.

At first, theirs was the perfect marriage. With demanding careers taking up most of their time, Megan and Tony didn't have many opportunities to enjoy each other's company. But when they did, they made sure that they spent their time—and money—in style. They bought a house in the Cayman Islands and flew there every year on a chartered private jet. They compensated themselves with watches and jewelry and new clothes. They hired a personal chef, a trainer, and a woman whose only job was to organize the closets in their enormous New York apartment.

And then the economy crashed.

For a while, Tony laughed the whole thing off, saying it was only a matter of time before the market righted itself and everything was back to normal. After a few months went by and more scandals erupted, things seemed to get bleaker and bleaker. His confidence waned and he suggested that they think of selling their Caribbean home. One evening, he came back home earlier than expected, poured himself a tall glass of scotch, and told his wife the awful news: his company was going under and he was now without a job.

Megan tried to be brave. "Surely," she told her hurting husband, "you'll find a new job in a few weeks, maybe a month or two at the very most. I still have my job and we have plenty of money to go around. I promise we'll be all right, Tony. This crisis will be over before we know it."

However, the crisis continued. Without Tony's enormous salary to sustain their lifestyle, the couple soon realized a crushing truth: like so many Americans, they were living way beyond their means. Even with tons of money coming in every month, they were spending nearly twice what they could afford. They had huge debts on their two homes—debts they couldn't possibly begin to pay off now that Tony was unemployed. They sold the house in the Caribbean for less than half of its cost. Two months later, they called a real estate broker and put their Manhattan apartment up for sale as well. It, too, was sold for far less than they had paid for it. Tony and Megan, once on top of the world, were now living in a small rented apartment more than a mile away from their former home in a chic downtown neighborhood—their fancy clothes cramped in tiny closets and their spirits lower than ever.

It didn't take long for the fighting to start. Almost nightly, Megan and Tony were at each other's throats, quibbling about who was more responsible for their financial mess—accusing each other, yelling at one another, and making life miserable. They now did everything they could to stay away from home—away from the unbearable tension of being together. Over Sunday brunch, Megan confided to a friend that she would love to divorce Tony—if only she had the money. Divorce lawyers were very expensive and she didn't have that kind of cash lying around. Her marriage, she cried, was over.

*   *   *

Eric was the kind of guy who did everything big. When he graduated from college, he rented out a boat and took all of his friends on a marvelous, memorable cruise. When he threw Super Bowl or Oscar parties, he would make specialty cocktails and colorful snacks and would give out small party favors. When he would date, Eric was at the top of his game.

Dinner and a movie were never enough. Or rather, they were enough if the movie was a red-carpet premiere and the dinner at a fancy, impossible-to-get-a-table kind of place. Otherwise, Eric was afraid that his date might not like him enough and would walk away disappointed, thinking that he wasn't making enough of an effort to woo her. Eric thought he was more likely to succeed if he mounted an elaborate, complicated production and made sure it was glittering and expensive.

One evening, hanging out with a few friends in a local bar, he met Rebecca. She was new to town, and knew one of Eric's friends from college. She had wide, almond-shaped eyes and long brown hair. When she laughed, she would throw her head back and let her entire body tremble with joy. Eric was smitten. Never a shy guy, he chatted her up and asked her out.

Eric's first date with Rebecca was a piece of theatre worthy of Broadway: using his connections, he managed to get a table at a Japanese restaurant that was so popular it demanded making reservations months in advance. He bought Rebecca a dozen white lilies and ordered the costly and elaborate tasting menu for them both. After dinner, he asked her to close her eyes and drove her to an upscale dance studio, where he had an instructor waiting to give the two of them a private tango lesson—Rebecca had mentioned that she was interested in the Argentinean dance. Then, it was off to a bar in the oldest and nicest hotel in town, where Eric ordered terrific port and told Rebecca he would very much like to see her again.

On her end, Rebecca was deeply impressed. She was a low-maintenance girl and expected nothing fancier than some pizza and cheap wine at a local joint. Many of her past boyfriends wouldn't even go as far as that—saving all of their money and energy for hanging out with friends or going on surfing trips. When Eric dropped her off at home that first night, she ran straight into her roommate's bedroom, flung herself on the bed, and gushed about what a perfect gentleman Eric was and how thrilled she'd be to see him again.

And see him again she did, very soon: he called the very next day to ask her out. Soon, they were seeing each other every two or three days. Their dates were just as stellar as that first one had been. Eric took Rebecca to concerts and plays, cooked her dinners, and bought her flowers and chocolates. A few weeks into their relationship, he even surprised her with a short weekend getaway to Mexico, where they stayed in an upscale hotel and spent their days lounging by the pool. Rebecca was soon in love—and so was Eric.

However, there were problems. While the decent money he made as a junior lawyer was more than enough for Eric to live nicely, he soon realized that the relationship was making him broke. He already owed a few thousand dollars on his credit card and, with the economy so tight and raises not forthcoming, he saw no way to get out of the slump. Talking to his best friend one weekend morning while working out, he came clean about his spending spree and asked his friend for a bit of advice. The friend was taken aback.

"You like Rebecca," he said, "and she likes you, so just sit her down and tell her that as much as you enjoy taking her to all these trendy places, you have no money right now and you need to cut back on your spending. If she truly likes you, she won't care."

Eric nodded but knew he just couldn't bring himself to follow his friend's sensible advice. He worried that if he didn't take Rebecca to great dinners and lovely vacations and interesting outings, she would gradually lose interest. He liked her too much to disappoint her now by telling her they couldn't do the sorts of things they had gotten used to doing.

Eric continued to spend and his financial situation continued to spiral out of control. It took a toll on him—once easy-going and relaxed, he was becoming increasingly tense and stressed out. Rebecca noticed but was afraid to say anything; if Eric wanted to tell her what was the matter, she thought, he would do so himself.

More months went by and more money was spent. Eric, now nearly $10,000 in debt, was a nervous wreck. Afraid to come clean to Rebecca, he said nothing. Going out with one of her colleagues one evening, she said she thought things were over between her and Eric. "He's always tense," she said, "and I'm pretty sure he wants to break up with me and doesn't know how."

*　　　*　　　*

Amy and Dan, Megan and Tony, Rebecca and Eric—all three are real couples. While they are very different in many ways—age, family, money—they have one major thing in common: like many Americans, they all fell victim to the recent economic crisis.

We don't mean to say that they simply found themselves with less income than before—that is obvious. What we're suggesting is something bigger, something more emotional, something that the thousands of news reports about the credit crunch and the subprime mortgage meltdown and the stimulus package neglected to mention: money goes hand in hand with love—and when one goes flying out the window, the other often does as well.

We know that this sounds strange. After all, the Beatles, those great philosophers, have already made it clear that money can't buy love and most of our greatest love stories focus on impoverished lovers who manage to come together despite the odds.

The truth, sadly, is more complicated: in a recent poll by Harris Interactive titled "Men, Love, and Sex," 38 percent of those asked—men and women alike—said that money was the number one cause for marital strife, far ahead of other culprits such as kid-related stress or sexual problems. According to this logic, the recent economic crisis seems like terrible news for anyone trying to keep a relationship going strong. If you were quibbling about cash when you had plenty of it, things are bound to get much harder now that you have much less. Right?

No.

Dead wrong.

At the heart of this book is one simple truth, and while it won't help you avoid the next economic meltdown or spot the next Bernie Madoff, it will help you save money and save your relationship. You can't afford to break up—and you don't need to. All you need to jump-start your love life is an empty wallet and a dirty mind. And we're pretty sure you've got both.

To kick things off, let's start with a few basic assumptions that are worth thinking about seriously:

♦ **All You Need Is Love:** Sure, that vacation in Las Vegas was grand and it was fun sipping cocktails on the beach in Aruba, but in all likelihood, these aren't the things that come to your mind when you think about your partner. Much more likely, you think about the way his eyes crinkle when he smiles or the way she cuddles up to you after you make love. You think about that one totally great, totally spontaneous evening when you had a slice, a few beers, and then went back home and had sex all night. You think about the little things, and the little things are the biggest things of all when it comes to relationships. The best thing? They're all free. So instead of moaning about how you can't afford to go to a nice dinner or take a lavish vacation, remember that these things you like best are right here—affordable and available—just as they've always been.

♦ **It's All In Your Head:** You don't need us to tell you that, do you? Everyone from Freud to Oprah has already said the same thing: every good romance, every great lay, every thrill always starts in your mind. Without imagination, even the most elaborate scenario falls flat, and with it, a bare room can turn into a truly exciting place. This is especially true in love: fantasies, daydreams, and dirty thoughts are a huge part of keeping a relationship fresh and fun. Oh, and did we mention they don't cost a dime?

♦ **Forever Young:** If we asked you to think of the last time you felt truly sexy, truly desirable, and truly free, we're willing to bet quite a bit of money that you'd say it was back in the day. Maybe it was in college or high school or when you had a bit more hair and a few less pounds, before kids and careers and the weight of life brought you down. Are we right? We think we are. The bad news is that we can't make you young again. The good news? We can remind you of one very important fact that you seem to be forgetting: you were *poor* back then! You had the energy but not the cash. So why is it that now, when times are tough financially, you seem to think that not having money is what's standing between you and happiness? After all, if you were poor and happy before, you can be poor and happy again.

♦ **Let's Talk About Sex, Baby:** Let us tell you something—sex is amazing. Revolutionary, right? We bet you haven't heard that one before. Nevertheless, it bears mentioning again and again, because it's important and it's often overlooked; there's no greater pleasure than getting naked with someone you deeply love, and there's no reason for even the most dire of circumstances to get in the way of mind-blowing, toe-curling, universe-expanding sex. Don't worry; we'll tell you all about it soon.

With these solid truths in mind, let us be a bit more blunt and cite once again the title of this book: *You Can't AFFORD to Break Up.* We know, it sounds depressing; after all, we'd all like to think that even when things are grim, we at least have the power to decide who we want to be with or not. But it's very true. That divorce lawyer you'll need to hire will cost you tens of thousands of dollars—not to mention the mess of splitting up the assets in these economically uncertain times. That affair you're going to have—we're not even talking about morality here—is just too expensive, what with all the motel rooms in out-of-the-way places. Even the cost of finding a new partner—you know, all that wining and dining that are a must for courtships—is cost-prohibitive. Right now, you can't afford any of these things.

The good news is that you don't have to. You don't need a new relationship. You've already got one. It may be a bit tattered or a bit strained, but with some fixing, it can be saved—and it can go a long way. Isn't saving just what we're supposed to do in tough economic times?

We're kidding, of course, but only a little bit. While we truly believe that breaking up is a difficult financial decision in these rough times, we also believe it's a tough decision emotionally—at least more often than not. We don't want to sound too sentimental here, but there was a time, not so long ago, when people stayed together, when they braved these crises that plague every marriage and made it work. Families may not have been perfect, but at least they stayed together. While we're not advocating that anyone remain in a relationship that they feel is not good for their bodies, their minds, or their souls, we think that a little patchwork can go a long way toward making things work out. With a little work, you can stay together and be happy.

How do we know? To answer that question, let us return to our three couples.

Remember Dan and Amy? After the fighting got unbearable, they left the kids with her mother and took a long weekend together in a nearby lakeside resort. They talked everything over and, the more they talked, the more they realized that the economic crunch didn't have to destroy them. It could even be something that brought them *closer* together—a challenge demanding every ounce of creativity they had. They're still working hard at it, but things are much better than they used to be.

Tony and Megan also had some pretty tough times and, at one point, Tony even left the apartment and spent more money that he didn't have on a hotel room for a couple of nights. He did come back and had a very difficult, very honest talk with Megan. They decided they wanted to be together and that while it was sure nice having fancy cars and nice houses, it was each other they truly loved—not their stuff. They gave it another shot and found out that their romance was as passionate and fun as it has ever been.

And Eric and Rebecca? They finally had the talk that Eric had dreaded so much. He told her he didn't have any money and that they couldn't go out for a long while. He told her how deeply sorry and how truly ashamed he was—and she laughed.

"I was sure you were about to dump me," she said, "and I'm very relieved to hear it's only about money."

They hugged, resolved to live frugally, and continued to have an evening of fun—eating canned soup and having hot sex. They are happier than they've ever been.

Three miracles, you say? Unlikely to happen to you? Too rosy, too impossible, too ridiculous? Not at all. These three real-life couples stayed together—they each found, in fact, that their relationship is as strong as it has ever been—because they didn't let the tough times get the better of them. They took the crisis as an opportunity to get back to basics and to rediscover the things that truly matter. They were proactive and used their imaginations to be sexy and have fun.

This short book will teach you to do the same thing. Since one of us is a therapist and the other a Hollywood actress, trust us that we know all you need to know about relationships, about talking, about sex, and about how to make it all work out.

Our approach is simple. It's right there in the subtitle of this book: all you need is an empty wallet and a dirty mind (hopefully, this is something you'll always have).

If you can use your imagination, if you can fantasize, if you can talk, you can have a great life, amazing sex, and a terrific relationship, no matter what your monthly bank statement says. To teach you how to do that, we have divided the book into several chapters:

- ♦ **Chapter One—Talk Is Cheap:** Talking is at the heart of every relationship. It's the first stage in every courtship and the first step of every romance. But talking ain't easy: most of us find talk—honest, open, sexy talk—to be very difficult to achieve, and succumb to shame, anxiety, or fear. Unless it's talk *during* sex, we find talking about sex, or about relationships, or about what we really want deep down inside to be almost impossible. This chapter will help you learn how to know yourself and how to talk to your partner. It will begin with a segment about learning how to come to terms with yourself—mentally, spiritually, and sexually—embracing your sexual past, and being clear and open about your sexual likes and dislikes. Once this is in place, it's time to talk to your partner; we'll suggest a few techniques for doing that, including a fun and sexy questionnaire that will help the two of you get more open and more forthcoming than you've probably ever been before. The more openly you learn how to communicate, the easier it will be to overcome your hurdles, to get to know your partner's past and sensibility, and to establish a direct and honest intimacy.

- ♦ **Chapter Two—All the World's A Stage:** And so, you learned to talk honestly. But talk isn't enough: now it's time to act. Literally: using techniques learned over years in the business, we will give you a down-and-dirty guide to using fantasy, acting, and the power of the imagination to inject your relationship with variety and excitement. This chapter will teach you how to get into character, how to write a mini-script you can enact in the bedroom, how to use props, and everything else you need to make your love life, well, dramatic.

- ♦ **Chapter Three—Shiny, Happy People:** Like it or not, you and your partner are not the only people in the world. Everywhere you go, people check you out, tease, and flirt. Instead of being jealous or throwing a fit and making your partner feel guilty for being an attractive, sexual human being, we'll teach you how to safely and securely harness this energy and channel it back into your bedroom. Guided by our therapist, we'll teach you how that stranger hitting on you in a bar or that person chatting you up at the gym can turn into the subject of foreplay between you and your partner, can get your hormones stirring, and can spice things up while staying safely within the boundaries of the relationship.

- ♦ **Chapter Four—Can't Buy Me Love:** Your mother probably told you when you were growing up that the two things you must never talk about in polite society are politics and religion. We agree, but would like to add two more: sex and money. Only guess what—sex and money actually make great conversation topics. They are two of the most raw, explosive topics around. Handled insensitively, they can leave us hurt and angry, but approached in the right way, they can drive us wild with desire. This chapter will focus on the emotional connections between your finances and your romance, teaching you how to overcome feelings of sexual inadequacy brought about by financial loss, how to channel the passions unleashed by the market into the bedroom, and how to make financial compatibility—a crucial component, most experts agree, of a successful marriage—synonymous with sexual chemistry.

We hope you like the way this sounds. After all, you can't afford not to nowadays. Since this book is geared toward couples in all stages of their relationship and in all kinds of economic situations, here's a fun little quiz you can take to help you identify where you and your partner are:

1. If my relationship was a car, it would surely be a:

a. Jalopy: it was awesome when it was new, but it's been around the block a couple of hundred of times, and now it's falling apart. It's probably best just to junk it.

b. Station Wagon: nothing thrilling about it and it's kind of used, but it's still dependable. It still does the job of getting me from place A to place B—I guess I'll keep it until something better comes along.

c. Sports Car: it's brand new. It's shiny. It moves really, really fast. Sure, safety may be a concern, but for now I'm just digging the excitement.

2. Look at my bank statement and you'll find:

a. A blank page. Seriously. Nothing describes my non-existent money better than a blank page.

b. Some numbers. I'm not filthy rich, but I have a bit squared away and, barring major disasters, I should be all right.

c. An epic poem. My many holdings and investments take a long time to go through, but I'm so wealthy I don't even bother trying.

3. When my partner and I talk, it sounds like:

a. A haiku: short and often hard to understand.

b. A newspaper: nothing too thrilling but conveys all the necessary information.

c. A rock ballad: long! Drenched with emotion! Awesome!

4. My idea of great sex involves:

a. Not having it. By the time I get home from work, I'd rather hang out with Ben & Jerry's than with my partner. If I make it into the bed, I fall asleep right away. I know it's not thrilling, but that's life, buster.

b. The usual stuff. Give me a bottle of wine, some flowers, a candle, maybe, and I'll be set. I'm really happy when I'm with someone I love, and it doesn't take much to get me in the mood.

c. Leather, maybe, or a waterbed, or fifteen spectators, or the risk of getting caught. You get the point: I don't like vanilla and I prefer my sex to be dripping with danger and excitement.

5. Finally, when I think about sex and money, I:

a. Scratch my head. I just don't see the connection between the two.

b. Squirm in my chair. I'm not comfortable talking about these things.

c. Get all excited. After all, these are highly charged topics we're talking about.

We hope this gives you a good idea of what's in store. Just remember that you can't afford to break up. You're going to save your relationship. You're going to save money. You have everything you need to be happy again. All you need is an empty wallet and a dirty mind. All you need is love—and *a lot* of sex, too. Have fun.

If you answered three or more questions with the letter:

a. You've got some serious work to do! Read this book as if it is the Bible.   Read it! Take notes! And reread it again!

b. Not bad, but if you want to spice up your life, this book can kick everything into a higher gear.

c. You guys are rocking! This book will give you some pointers to keep those home fires burning!

d.

Chapter One—Talk Is Cheap

Amy was frustrated. A few years and a couple of kids into the marriage, things between her and Dan were getting sort of stale. When it was just the two of them living in their small, stylish Chicago apartment, romance came easily. But now, in the suburbs, with two girls to feed and dress and drive around, with careers and responsibilities, and with the economy making things tighter than ever, being romantic seemed like a luxury they couldn't afford.

They still went on dates, but they were few and far between. They still had sex, but it happened too infrequently. They were still in love, but mostly they were just tired, anxious, and stressed out.

Having coffee with a girlfriend one afternoon, Amy couldn't keep it in any longer. She told her friend everything and confessed that she felt that her marriage might not survive if things continued that way. She asked for advice; the friend suggested a romantic dinner and sexy lingerie. It sounded tacky, Amy thought to herself, but she had nothing to lose.

A week or two later, she asked her mother to take the girls for an evening and told Dan to come home from work earlier than usual. When he walked into the house, he was surprised by what he saw: the lights were dimmed, smooth jazz music was playing softly on the stereo, and there were rose petals scattered on the hardwood floor. Before too long, Amy appeared wearing a tight dress and makeup. She walked over to him and, without saying a word, began kissing him passionately, grabbing his hair, and rubbing herself against his body.

Then Dan did the most terrible thing he could have done: he stepped back.

Amy was stunned. Why wasn't her husband responding to her advances? Why was he recoiling? She was deeply hurt and found it impossible not to sob. Dan muttered apologies: it wasn't that he didn't want to make love to her and it wasn't that he didn't appreciate her efforts, but he needed a few minutes after coming home from work—a few minutes to unwind and relax before he could seriously get in the mood. He walked over to Amy and tried to fondle her. Still sobbing, she ran upstairs to their bedroom.

Dan followed her, still apologizing. He didn't mean it like that, he said. She had to forgive him. Still, Amy continued to cry, saying nothing, and Dan, nervous, talked on.

"You know," he told his wife, "it's just the way I am. I need time to forget about work and start thinking about you. Also, I love that you took the time to do all this for us, but if we're already being honest here, I don't really like all that flower and jazz stuff. It's too soft for me. I prefer to feel a little bit dirty—like we're doing something that's not straight out of a romantic movie. Something more sexy—maybe even a bit naughty. Forget the flowers—how about we go do it outside in the yard? It's dark, and I don't think anybody will see us. And if they do, then I say let 'em."

Amy wasn't crying anymore. She was listening. She had no idea her husband felt that way. She'd always thought that a bit of lingerie and some smooth music was all it took to get him in the mood—and yet here he was with this exhibitionist fantasy. Still, she was turned on: the thought of making love outside, on the neatly cut grass of their back yard, under the big sky in the perfect spring weather was extremely appealing. She didn't want to waste any more time. She got up, looked her husband in the eye, undressed, and walked down the stairs and into the yard. Dan did the same. They were about to have a night to remember.

*   *   *

It was one o'clock in the morning, and Megan was sitting in the kitchen, crying. She and Tony had just had another big fight, and he'd stormed out of the apartment, slamming the door behind him. It was the same as so many evenings they'd had recently: coming home from work tense and tired, eating dinner in silence, trying awkwardly to find something to talk about, and somehow ending up screaming at each other, angry and often tearful.

Megan reached for her pack of cigarettes. Her hands shaking, she fished one out and lit it up. She couldn't take it anymore—the constant quibbling with her husband and the invisible wall that seemed to have sprung up between them these last several months. Sure, times were tough: Tony had lost his job and they were forced to sell their apartment, move to a cramped rental, and give up their previously luxurious lifestyle. But plenty of people were in the exact same situation, she told herself in between drags, plenty of couples now found themselves without jobs and homes and security—and not all of them fought all the time. Or did they? Megan wasn't sure. She was sad, and angry, and awash in self-pity. She had no idea what to do.

A friend recommended a yoga retreat. Another suggested couples' therapy. A third said taking a long vacation together might be a good idea. But all of these things cost money and money was just what Megan and Tony didn't have. Frustrated, they did nothing. The tension continued. Things got worse.

Then, one night, it all came to a head.

It started out just like any other night: when Megan came home from work, Tony was lying on the couch watching a ball game on TV. They pecked each other on the cheek, asked about each other's day, and ordered Chinese food. The conversation came to money. When Megan said something, Tony took it as an attack on him and snapped at her. Megan barked back and soon they were at each other's throats. Again, Tony got up to leave. Before he did, however, he turned to his wife and, his eyes wet with tears and his body quivering with rage, hissed a single question at her: "What do you want?" he asked. "Exactly what do you want?"

He slammed the door behind him again, but this time Megan wasn't looking for her smokes. She had just had an epiphany. Tony meant it as a rhetorical question—one of those things people say when they're angry—but Megan thought he made an excellent point: just what *did* she want? After all, she had spent the previous months talking about what she *didn't* want: she didn't want to stress out about money, she didn't want to have to think about every dollar she spent, and she didn't want to go on like this—with no economic security and no good financial plan for the future. But what did she want? That was an entirely different question.

She poured herself a glass of wine and started thinking about it. The first answers that came to mind were obvious. She wanted Tony to find a job. So did he, but there wasn't much they could do about it in such an awful market. She wanted a bigger apartment, wanted to buy back the house in the Caribbean, wanted a new car and jewelry, and wanted to be able to sleep in peace without worrying about money all the time. All of these things, she realized, were not under her control.

What else, she asked herself, what else did she want? Or rather, what did she want that she could actually get and could actually afford? A backrub would be lovely, she mumbled to herself, laughing; it seemed so ridiculous to go from thinking about luxury homes to something as simple and ordinary as a backrub.

Then it hit her.

A backrub would be terrific. Not as terrific as financial stability and economic security, but terrific. It would make her feel better—maybe only for a few hours—but better nonetheless. It wouldn't solve any of her life problems, but it would put a whole new spin on the evening. She grabbed her cell phone and called Tony. Come home, she told him, there's something very important I'd like you to do. When he returned a few minutes later, she was sitting on the couch, smiling.

"Rub my back," she pleaded.

Tony stared at his wife. Had she gone crazy? One minute she's talking about mutual funds and 401(k)s and the next about massages? Still, he walked over to Megan, sat beside her, and started to gently caress her neck. An hour later, they were on the bed, making love, laughing, and holding each other. It was the best evening they'd had in a very long time.

*   *   *

"What?" cried Eric, agitated.

"Nothing," Rebecca said angrily, pulling up the blanket to cover her naked body. "Forget it. I'm going to bed. Good night."

It was Saturday and they had just come back from a fun dinner. They'd shared a bottle of wine and a few cocktails beforehand, so by the time they stumbled back into Rebecca's apartment, they were delightfully drunk. They had been dating for only a few months and this was, by far, the part they most enjoyed about the whole courtship ritual: going out, making out in the cab on the way back home, and then jumping into bed for a night of passion. And that night seemed no different.

But then, Eric ruined everything. He started talking.

They were just past foreplay, their clothes mostly off, when he started asking Rebecca questions. He wanted her to tell him everything, he said, how she liked to be touched and where and how softly. At first, she laughed it off.

"Find out for yourself," she said, "don't be a lazy bum." But he was persistent: exploring her body, he stopped every few moments to look up at her and seek her approval.

"Don't worry about it," she said, "it feels great, just kiss me."

But Eric wanted her to talk and to walk him through every single one of her likes and dislikes, but she was not in the mood for all that talking. Finally, she couldn't take it any longer and told him to stop. He was offended; she was flustered. They both went to bed angry.

But Rebecca couldn't fall asleep. At three in the morning, she woke Eric up, tearful. She was sorry, she said, but she just didn't know how to talk about these things frankly. She would tell him, she promised, she would tell him all about her fantasies and passions and peeves—she would tell him if she could. But Rebecca wasn't sure that *she* even knew everything. They would need to learn it together.

*   *   *

Before we go any further, we'd like to take a moment to quote a bit of ancient Greek philosophy. We know, you didn't buy this book expecting to read about Plato or Socrates and we won't bore you with too many unnecessary details. In fact, we're going to keep it very simple. There's only one bit of wisdom we'd like you to consider, a bit of wisdom that summarizes much of Greek thought in two words: know yourself.

Whether you're thinking about money or marriage or sex or love or dinner or the New York City Marathon, this is an excellent piece of advice. Every action you ever take—every commitment or agreement or pursuit—should begin with real, honest self-knowledge. If you don't start with this, you'll run into trouble. If you do, you will prevail. It's that simple. They may have worn togas and gorged themselves with food until they puked, but about some things the ancient Greeks were very, very smart.

But we're not here to talk about the ancient Greeks. We're here to talk about your relationship and how you can save it—especially now that tough economic times are taking their terrible toll. We'd like to begin by talking about the one person who can do the most to help you get out of the slump and rekindle your romance. That person, of course, is you.

Let us ask you a question that may sound ridiculous at first: how well do you know yourself? If you were suddenly given a pop quiz on your life, how well would you do? We don't mean the obvious things such as when and where were you born and what was your mother's maiden name, the kind of trivia that your bank may set up as a security question when you log on to your account. We're talking about the bigger things—the things that truly matter. If we gave you fifteen seconds, for example, and complete confidence, could you tell us what you really love that your partner does during sex? Would you be able to say what it is that your partner likes most about you and what it is that he or she likes least? Would you be able recall your happiest moment or your saddest?

Please, don't feel bad if the answer to any or all of these questions is no. We suspect most people couldn't. That's the tragedy—we're always told that it's important to be honest and open and communicative, but we're never told how to communicate or what we should be open and honest about. That was what got Amy and Dan, Megan and Tony, and Rebecca and Eric into trouble: they just didn't know themselves well enough, or how to talk to each other, and the moment they figured it out, things took a turn for the better. Without self-realization, mutual communication, and open interaction, nothing positive can ever grow.

Our goal in this chapter, then, is to give you some tools to help you learn more about yourself and how to talk to your partner about your needs, passions, and fears. The two are closer than you think—sometimes you learn the most intimate and incredible things about yourself only when you talk to someone else. Sometimes a realization you've made on your own that paves the road to a healthy relationship. What we're saying, then, is that getting to know yourself—and getting to know your partner—is a process. It takes time and it takes work. Parts of it are meant as a solitary exercise and parts are designed to do together.

Where, then, to begin? Simple. We begin with you and where you've been. Don't worry; we're not going to wax poetic about it. Instead, we'd like to give you a very concrete exercise. Here goes:

To complete this assignment properly, we'll need you to take an afternoon off—or at least steal away a few hours on the weekend or in the evening. We want you to be relaxed and unencumbered by scheduling and stuff you have to do. We want you to clear your mind.

Begin, then, by doing just that. Have a glass of wine, maybe, or indulge in a favorite snack. Stretch, be comfortable; after all, we're going to ask you to travel to places you haven't visited in a very long time.

Ready? Let's go. We need you to take a sheet of paper and a pen, and start preparing what we call your Personal Emotional Passport, or PEP. It's a document only you will ever see—so be very honest with yourself.

1. The first stage of filling out your PEP is simple: on one side of the page, list ten times you've felt happy and on the other, ten times you've felt miserable. We know, we know, we're being very vague. There's the sort of happiness you feel when you listen to a song you like and then there's the sort of happiness you feel on your wedding day. The same goes for sadness. So which should you focus on? Whichever you want. The point of this exercise is not to think—just write down whatever comes to mind. Since *not* thinking is precisely the point, we don't want you to spend too much time making this list. It shouldn't take more than five minutes.

2. When you're done, however, the hard work begins. Now it's time to make sense of it all. Read every item on the list carefully and slowly, alternating between good and bad experiences.

3. Close your eyes, and try to relive each moment: what was it about that particular instant that made you joyous or unhappy? Were your feelings

the result of other people's behaviors or were they all of your own making? And what did it feel like—physically *feel* like—at the moment? The more deeply you manage to place yourself back in that same situation, the more likely you are to understand it—and the more you understand it, the better your chances of understanding your emotions. It makes perfect sense: if you understand perfectly what it was that made you very happy once before, you're very likely to be able to channel that same feeling again.

And speaking of feeling, don't be afraid to get very specific and very sexual. Here, for example, are a few quick and easy thought experiments. Try answering these questions:

- *Without thinking too much, what was the most thrilling sexual experience of your life?*
- *Now, take the time to think; why did you reply as you did? What was so special about that experience?*
- *What turns you on? Is there a specific scenario that's recurrent in your fantasies?*
- *Is there a particular type of person you're attracted to?*
- *Which of the five senses plays the biggest role in turning you on?*
- *Write your own letter to* Penthouse Forum *and describe a specific fantasy that turns you on. Be as specific as possible.*

This, of course, is a very general approach. To truly know everything about yourself and about where you've been, you'll need to repeat a separate PEP exercise for every aspect of your history—from your career to your love life. At the end of this chapter, we'll provide you with a questionnaire that may make things easier. In the meantime, we want you to get busy thinking about where you've been in life—emotionally, sexually, and mentally—because there's no other way to know who you are and where you're going. Don't abandon your PEP once your alone time is over. Continue to think about yourself and about your past. You'll find that it's fascinating stuff.

Hey, we know that some of this is really heavy. So to jumpstart your journey to self-realization, we've put together a few basic pointers to help guide you along your way.

♦ **Be Honest.** Remember that this is you that you're talking to. You already know all of your secrets, so there's no point in holding back. It's possible that what's really bothering you is something unpleasant—or even dark—but without confronting it head-on, you're never likely to begin resolving the issue.

♦ **Be Physical.** Don't just ask yourself what you think about a given topic—ask how it makes you feel. Try to close your eyes and imagine how whatever it is you're thinking about might look and smell and how it might make your body react. The brain's an important organ, but it's not our only one, and we shouldn't let it dictate the way we get to know ourselves. Get into your body and feel it.

♦ **Be Imaginative.** Talking about the PEP, we encouraged you to make a list of things that have happened to you. But there's another list, equally as important, that you should think about: a list of things you *wish* happened to you. We're not just talking big lottery wins or Miss America—although those would be nice—but a list of situations where you would like to see yourself before too long. Top-notch athletes often speak of visualizing a certain important play during a big game, imagining it in their heads before they can carry it out with their bodies. The same is true for the rest of us.

♦ **Be Constructive.** Using your imagination is great and thinking lofty thoughts is fine, but you need to make sure this exercise in getting to know yourself isn't wasted. Remember that these are tough economic times and everything you do must serve a purpose. So when you think, think constructively. Think about little things that can be done to improve your life, to brighten your days, and to correct some of your bad habits. Don't sweat the small stuff—change it: the small stuff can be as small as trying to stop swearing, to picking up the clothes you throw on the floor at the end of the day and drive your partner mad, or resolving to treat yourself to a brief bubble bath once a week. These things add up.

All right, enough about you. After all, you didn't buy this book just to learn about yourself. You bought it because you wanted to learn how to save your relationship and how to make it thrive. Now it's time to begin doing just that—by talking to your partner.

If we had to pick the single most misunderstood notion in relationships, it would be that it's really important to talk to each other openly and honestly. Every therapist will tell you that—and every advice book will repeat it again and again. However, what they often neglect to tell you is that talking is really, really hard. It's not as if we can just sit down, open our mouths, and eloquently express our innermost sentiments. Often, we don't even know ourselves what it is that we want to say and, even when we do, it's difficult to put it in a way that will make much sense to another human being who wants and thinks and feels completely different things.

How many times, for example, did you have a very specific wish for a very particular birthday gift in mind, but when your partner asked you what present you'd like to receive, you shrugged and said nothing? Come on, we all do it. And we do it because we don't want to tell our partners what we want—we want them to guess. And we want them to guess just the right thing. We want them to know us telepathically—without talking. We think it's more romantic. We're kind of crazy that way.

We're not going to tell you to just do it because we know how hard talking can be. We're going to give you a few pointers and guidelines to help you along. We hope that by the time you're done reading this chapter, you'll have a much better idea of how to complete the first step in saving your relationship—by establishing an open channel of communication.

To get things started—and keeping in mind the dire economic times—we're going to suggest one of the greatest, most fun, and totally free activities out there: watching TV. Even if one of you likes sports and the other is into soap operas, there must be at least one program you both enjoy. Get on that couch, snuggle, and tune in.

As you watch, however, we'd like you to suggest a little game to your partner. It's called "Who Would You Be?" Wait for a boring moment in the plot, or for a commercial break, and ask your partner which character he or she imagines they would be if he or she were in the show. Would they choose the sexy, seductive doctor who has trouble sticking to long-term relationships? Or do they see themselves as the brilliant but emotionally brittle cop who needs constant attention? Television is great like that: it gives us so many characters and we can look at those characters and try to find in them a little bit of ourselves. It may sound silly at first, but it allows us to talk about ourselves while pretending we're really talking about fictional characters. Once you've heard your partner's choice, and shared your own, spend a little while talking about why the both of you responded as you did—and what your selections tell you about yourselves and each other. Presto: all the benefits of an open and honest conversation with none of the hassle.

Eventually, of course, we recommend the good ol' fashioned type of talk—the one with two people sitting across from one another and addressing real emotions, hopes, and fears. In a few pages, we'll provide you with a detailed questionnaire to send you on your way to just such a conversation. Before you start talking, however, there are a few points you should consider—a few potential pitfalls that nab us all at one point or another and how to avoid them:

♦ **Curiosity, not Criticism**. So here you are, on the couch, and your partner says something that you find outrageous. Maybe even something about you. You get an urge—a physical yearning—to say something, to respond, or maybe even to retaliate. Relax: this isn't what talking is about. Treat everything your partner says as if you were a talk show host who is deeply fascinated by each one of his or her guest's comments and put away that urge to criticize, evaluate, or judge. You'll learn more about your partner and put him or her at ease, which is always good for the conversation. It's not easy, but it is essential.

♦ **Talk from the I Position, not the U position**. We're not talking about some kinky sex maneuvers here—just the elementary building blocks of conversation. Before you even sit down at the table or on the couch, tell yourself this: I am the only person that I know how to talk about. Anytime you feel yourself about to launch a "U" sentence—as in "you don't know what it feels like to be me" or "you have no idea what I've been through"—stop. Immediately. Rephrase that sentence. Drop the "U," and try an "I" instead, like "I feel this" or "I've been through that." You'll find that your sentences get better that way—more honest and more meaningful—and your partner will respect you for it and listen better when not being attacked.

♦ **Roger That**. Here's another rule of conversation: begin by acknowledging that you've heard what your partner has just said. Furthermore, repeat it. Two good things will happen: first of all, your partner will feel grateful and secure that you're actually paying attention. Second, they'll be able to hear your take on what they said, and make sure that you understood them correctly. Imagine that: a conversation without any misunderstandings. We promise you, this makes a huge difference.

♦ **Feelings Are Out of Bounds**. This one is simple: never argue with anyone's feelings. Your partner may tell you he or she feels that you behave a certain way, or that you don't love them anymore, or even that you may be a Martian secretly stowed away on earth. Don't argue. *Feel* is a funny word—unlike *think* or *know*—there's very little we can do with *feel* except for acknowledge it and try to amend our behavior accordingly. Accept it, understand it, and move on.

Finally, a word about sex. We know, we know: it isn't easy to talk about, and it can be especially hard sometimes to be frank with your partner about your sexual histories. Let's get real here: most of us have had other loves before our current partner—just as we've had other friends and other hobbies and other lives. It's totally normal and natural. Our sexual history makes up a large part of who we are, so it's important never to neglect it. We must talk about it. By bringing our sexual histories into the bedroom—perhaps not all at once and perhaps with minor edits inserted for all sorts of reasons—we can open previously unavailable lines of communication, increase our intimacy, and get to know each other better. Ignoring our sexual history because we fear it might make our partner jealous or angry or embarrassed deprives us of a large part of who we are. And that, we don't have to tell you, is bad.

You may be getting a bit tired of all this talk about talk, but we haven't even told you the best part yet: talk isn't just cheap—it's *free*. It's a way to get to know yourself, get to know your partner, fix so much of what is broken in your relationship, build a better life and more promising future, and do all that without spending a single cent. You really can't beat it.

So, to help you get started, we've devised a little questionnaire for you. It's a variation on a very famous quiz, made popular by the French writer Marcel Proust, which is now used by everyone from James Lipton on *Inside the Actor's Studio* to *Vanity Fair*. We've made our tweaks, of course, and invite you to make your own, as well. But the spirit of the quiz remains unchanged: it's a tool to better know someone—be it yourself or your partner—and once you get your answers, keep asking: there's no limit to what you can find out.

Knowing Me, Knowing You: A Quick Quiz about Almost Everything That Matters

♦ The quality I admire most about a member of the opposite sex is

- The thing I like most about myself is
- The thing I like least about myself is
- My idea of happiness is
- My idea of misery is
- The flaw for which I have the most tolerance is
- The flaw for which I have the least tolerance is
- My perfect date with a partner would consist of
- I think love is
- If I weren't myself, I'd like to be
- The nicest thing anyone has ever said to me was
- The most hurtful thing anyone has ever said to me was
- Something I'd always be willing to spend a lot of money on is
- Something I'd never be willing to spend a lot of money on is
- Other than the necessary stuff, I believe a monthly budget should also allow for
- If I could give up one thing to make my partner happy, it would be
- If my partner could give up one thing to make me happy, I'd like it to be
- If I had to describe myself in just one word, it would be
- If I had to describe my partner in just one word, it would be
- My real-life hero is
- A talent I wish I had is
- If I could give my partner any gift, I'd choose
- The one thing I'll never forgive my partner for is
- The thing I like most about my appearance is
- The thing I like least about my appearance is

- ♦ The thing I like most about my partner's appearance is
- ♦ The thing I like least about my partner's appearance is
- ♦ My greatest sexual fantasy is
- ♦ The thing that turns me off the most in a member of the opposite sex is
- ♦ What always gets me in the mood is
- ♦ If I weren't with my partner, a celebrity I'd love to spend the night with is
- ♦ My greatest regret is
- ♦ I consider my greatest achievement in life to be
- ♦ My motto in life is
- ♦ My current state of mind is

- ♦ Instructions: Think. Respond. Share. Repeat.

The Five Mantras of the Recession:

Sex is better than cash.

I was poor when I was young. I had fun then;
I'll have fun now.

Make love, not stock predictions.

Recessions come and go. Relationships stay.

The best things in life are free.

Chapter Two—All the World's a Stage

"For God's sake, Amy, I'm sick of having this argument again and again and again. If you don't want to come, just stay home."

With that, Dan stomped upstairs to the bedroom. Amy, still sitting on the couch, was a little bit shocked and very hurt. There was no reason, she thought, for Dan to snap at her like that; all she had done was suggest that this year, she might sit out his annual office party. She thought it was no big deal: every year, the employees of Dan's firm got together in their office's conference room, where a few balloons and cheap holiday decorations could barely make the office furniture and bright halogen lights look any more festive. They drank cheap white wine, snacked on stale cookies and nuts bought in bulk for the occasion by the office's thrifty manager at a local discount supermarket, and listened to kitschy holiday music blaring out through the tinny speakers of a beat up, ancient boom box. In short, it was not a fun night and Amy would have been perfectly happy to sit it out.

She would have been happy to go, of course, if she thought it was important to Dan, but he, too, dreaded the annual party. As early as October, he would moan and groan and say how much he'd love to just not show up and how he would gladly skip the whole thing if he didn't know it meant the world to John, the party's organizer and Dan's direct boss.

For the first few years of their marriage, Amy was glad to be there by Dan's side, thinking that it was her duty to keep her husband company in such an awful, mandatory affair. But every year, the same pattern occurred: as soon as they would arrive at the party, Dan would excuse himself and spend the entire evening chatting with his coworkers, leaving Amy stranded and annoyed. She would have talked to one of the other spouses, of course, but there never seemed to be too many of them around. John's wife, an elderly woman with a perpetual frown and clothes that looked as if they were made in the eighteenth century, was always there, but with the exception of one or two wives and two or three husbands, the party seemed to be strictly for company employees.

The first year Amy gently suggested skipping the party, Dan frowned and she quickly changed her mind, enduring a crushingly boring evening. The next year, she asked again, and again Dan frowned. This year, however, she wasn't going to let him off the hook easily: if he wanted her to come to the party with him, he at least had to explain to her why he needed her there if he had no intention of spending any time with her and planned on leaving her, as he always did, at the mercy of Cynthia, John's prudish wife. A week or two before the party, she confronted him. He erupted in anger and she was left on the couch, confused.

The next morning, Dan and Amy mumbled muffled apologies to one another but said nothing of the party. The days went by, but the party was not discussed. When the day finally arrived, Dan, sounding resigned and a bit sad, told his wife he would be late that night; the party was tonight and she didn't have to go, but he had no choice and would have to attend for John's benefit. He kissed her briefly on the cheek and left for the office.

At around six in the evening, all the employees of Dan's firm shut down their computers, left their desks, and shuffled off to the conference room. The same old dreary balloons floated over a few bottles of wine and tasteless snacks that were piled on a large rectangular table. Dan felt a light stab in the chest: he realized why Amy didn't want to come and realized that he had neglected her—year after year—making no effort to entertain her or make the party pleasant for her in any way. Yet, at that moment, he wished for nothing more than to be able to glance over to the corner, where John's wife was standing alone, to see his gorgeous wife smiling at him. Just that would make the whole dreadful evening so much better.

The evening dragged on and on. The same bad music and bad food and bad wine. The sharp sensation in Dan's chest grew stronger. He missed Amy terribly and was just about to leave the party and rush home to her when he saw a woman walk in through the door.

She wore a very red, very tight dress that highlighted every feature of her great body. Her hair was perfectly done and fell down on her forehead in rich, brown locks. She made her way elegantly and assuredly through the room; even though she wore long, sharp heels, she walked as gracefully and as naturally as if she had been barefoot.

Like those clichéd scenes in bad movies, it seemed to Dan that the music had screeched to a halt and everybody had stopped talking mid-sentence and gawked at the strange woman. Dan sure did. A moment or two later, he felt another strong sensation in his chest. This time, however, it was pure joy: the lady in red, he realized, was Amy.

She walked right up to him and handed him her purse. "Hold that, darling, would you?" she asked in a voice that was much deeper than her usual tone. "And get me a drink; I'm just dying for some chardonnay." Overwhelmed, Dan obeyed. As he walked over to the table to grab a drink for his wife, he looked at her some more and decided she looked and behaved just like a glamorous 1940s movie star—a Dietrich or a Garbo—with that sexy outfit and that sultry tone. He walked back and handed her the wine. She took it without saying a word, as she was deep in conversation with Todd and Ben, Dan's two closest friends at the office. Dan thought they were a tough duo—very shy and never too welcoming of people who weren't close friends or long-time colleagues. But at that moment, they seemed to be hanging on Amy's every word, looking at her admiringly. This, Dan realized, had never happened before.

And so it continued all of that night, Amy hopping from one colleague to another, introducing herself, speaking in that low, seductive voice and leaving Dan to chase her around the room, confused, doing his best to capture her attention. Dan couldn't wait for the evening to end; all he wanted was to be alone with his wife.

When they were finally alone, in their bedroom, having driven their separate cars back home, Dan had a million questions to ask Amy. *Where did she get that dress?*

And what was with the voice? And what was that charade all about?

But looking at her closely for a moment or two, he didn't need to ask a single question. He now understood everything, understood how his wife put on this performance that transformed her into someone else for a little bit, made him desire her desperately, and made even a dreary evening such as an office party an occasion for flirtation and romance.

Dan grabbed the lady in red and pulled her to him. It was time to make love to his own private movie star.

*   *   *

Megan stared blankly at the envelope on the table in front of her. She didn't open it. She knew what was inside and had no desire to read that one particular letter.

The identity of the sender was obvious: the logo on the envelope—large and colorful—made it clear that the sender was one of New York's most prestigious theatre companies. Once upon a time—before Tony lost his job, before they were forced to move to the small and crammed apartment, before they began to think twice about every penny they spent—this particular theatre company was one of Megan's favorite luxuries. She always loved going to the theatre and, back in the good days when money was plentiful, they donated generously to a few companies, enjoying tickets to sold-out shows and invitations to swanky cocktail receptions with actors and playwrights.

These heady days, she realized, were over.

And yet, here was the envelope. Inside it, she knew, was a solicitation for cash. A few days before, she'd read in the *New York Times* that the company was planning a splashy Shakespearean production with three or four major movie stars in the leading roles. The envelope, she knew, contained an offer: write a check and you can hobnob with the celebrities and enjoy their stellar performances.

Quickly, Megan tore open the envelope. The letter featured the bold-faced names of the new play's stars, and then the bold-faced price tag: a minimum of $1,000 per person. She knew that there was no way that she and Tony would be able to afford it.

That night at dinner, Megan was especially quiet. Later on that evening, finding the envelope on the kitchen counter, Tony read the theatre company's letter and realized just why Megan was upset. It broke his heart. *If only I hadn't lost my job,* he thought, *I could buy her the tickets she wants so badly.* He waited until Megan fell asleep and then went online to search the web for affordable tickets. He could find none. Racked with guilt, he couldn't fall asleep. He knew he had to do something—and he had a few weeks to plan it all out. He had to give Megan a bit of theatre, he knew, even if he couldn't afford the expensive tickets.

The day of the play's premiere, Tony waited until his wife left for work and then sent a text message asking her to make sure she did not come home before seven o'clock. Megan was intrigued: what, she wondered, was Tony planning? She called him and asked if he had any special activities in mind for that evening, but he just chuckled and refused to reveal any details. Megan hung up the phone, feeling a warm rush of emotion flooding her body. Tony was usually what one may call the strong, silent type—not exactly a man given to secretive and grand romantic gestures. She couldn't stop glaring at her watch. All she wanted to do was get home and find out what Tony had done.

At seven o'clock sharp, Megan turned her key in the lock, opened the door, and stepped in. What she saw made her gasp.

The living room, which was normally strewn with Tony's copy of *The Wall Street Journal* and his dirty coffee mug—and sometimes even his gym socks—was completely lit by candles. All the furniture had been moved and the floor was covered by their large blue rug. In the middle of it all sat Tony, beaming. He was wearing a paper crown—the sort handed out to children at a popular fast food restaurant—and was draped in a red blanket.

"What's going on?" Megan asked, her voice breaking and tears rushing to her eyes.

Tony got up and gave his wife a hug. He couldn't get any tickets to see the play, he told her, and he felt sorry for not being able to treat her to the fancy premiere that she was accustomed to. He had decided to do the next best thing: he reached into his makeshift cape and pulled out a copy of the play. If they couldn't afford the tickets, he told Megan, they'd put on their own production. He'd play the prince—and she would play his doomed lover. Their version would be much more fun, he promised his laughing wife, motioning toward a bottle of cheap champagne, some massage oils, and other elements

Shakespeare most certainly never intended to award his tragic hero.

Soon, they were fondling and kissing on the rug—taking turns reading the play out loud and pouring each other more sparkly wine. They made love, read some more, and then made love again. It was, Megan thought, smiling when they slid into bed, the absolute best night at the theatre they'd ever had.

*   *   *

It was five in the afternoon and Eric had just gotten his eighth text message of the day. The first one came around nine, just as he was walking into his office; he didn't recognize the number and the message was sexy and a bit explicit. Eric chuckled: some woman, he thought, had probably made an embarrassing mistake, sending the racy message to him instead of to her boyfriend.

An hour later, however, another message came, and then another, one every hour, each one more and more steamy. Sometime shortly after noon, Eric texted back and politely wrote that he thought whoever it was who was sending these messages had the wrong number.

"No," popped up another message, right away. "I don't, Eric."

Eric was a frazzled and a little bit concerned. How did the stranger know his name? And it had to be a stranger, after all, as the phone number of anyone he knew was stored on his cell phone and would have come up on the screen had he recognized the caller. This was creepy, he thought; what if the woman texting him was some sort of crazy stalker?

As if reading his mind, the anonymous woman sent another text message. "Don't worry, Eric," she wrote. "And don't try to guess who I am. Just play along. It's going to be fun. I promise." Then, another message, a long one, in which the mystery woman described in some detail what she'd like Eric to do to her if they were both alone together and naked.

Eric looked up quickly from his desk, making sure none of his colleagues noticed him blush. And blush he did: here was this mystery woman—this woman, he thought, who wasn't his girlfriend—sending him sexy and seductive messages. It turned him on—there was no doubt about that—but it also made him feel guilty. *What,* he thought, *would Rebecca do if she found out about these?* How could he ever explain to her that he had nothing to do with the woman's attempts at seducing him?

Eric was now sweating uncomfortably. As much as he was aroused by the stranger's graphic sexual descriptions, all he could think about was Rebecca. Rebecca, he thought, who was so sweet and so lovely and who could never bring herself to write such smut as this. He would have to tell her, he decided. There was no way he was going to keep something so odd a secret. But she would probably be upset. Eric was nervous.

He met Rebecca later that evening at a small Italian restaurant not far from her house. As soon as he saw her walking through the door, his heart skipped a beat: she was wearing an elegant lavender sweater and had her hair up, her pretty face beaming at him. There was just no way he could bring himself to tell her about the text messages; he didn't want to shift her open smile to a suspicious frown. If he told her, he was sure that she would think that he was having an affair, was unfaithful, or that he was the kind of guy who flirted with other women even when he had a serious girlfriend. He sat silently through the meal, letting Rebecca do most of the talking, doing his best to look calm and engaged. However, in his mind, the text messages played over again and again, every raunchy word sending shocks throughout his entire body. By the time the dessert arrived, Eric worked out a strategy: he would tell Rebecca he was tired, kiss her goodnight, and go home, spending the rest of the evening rereading his strange messages and trying to figure out who could have sent them.

The check came, and Eric paid. Following his plan, he told Rebecca he was exhausted and had a hectic day at work the next day, and that, if she didn't mind, he'd just like to go home and get a good night's sleep. Rebecca nodded her head and said she understood. She got up to go the bathroom. As she made her way around the table, she stopped for a second, hunched over, and whispered something in Eric's ear.

It was the dirtiest line from the dirtiest text message he had received that day.

When Rebecca returned from the bathroom a minute or two later, she found Eric, stunned, sitting in the exact same position she had left him, his mouth still open, his jaw dropped. She patted his head lightly.

"Come." She leaned over once more and breathed softly into his ear. "Let's go home and reread those messages, shall we?"

Later—much later—she told him how she had used new software that let her mask her caller ID, and how she had planned the texting campaign for days, and how she was going to use her own number and sign her name but then thought that anonymous messages may be a bit more exciting. But that was much later; before it came lovemaking much like the kind described in the texts—passionate, intimate, and thrilling. Eric and Rebecca never looked at their cellular phones the same way again.

*   *   *

As the title of this chapter suggests, all the world's a stage. If we stop to think about it, we realize just how much of life is really good theatre: when we play sports or get married, when we go to church or go to court, even when we interview for a job, we wear outfits we would never usually wear otherwise and say things we would never otherwise say and do things we don't usually do. We act. We pretend. We follow a script.

But here's the fascinating bit: when it comes to dating, the first advice any expert is likely to give you is this: be yourself.

Let's stop and think about that one for a moment. No one, for example, is saying you should just be yourself when you sit across the desk from a potential new employer. On the contrary: most people would tell you to put on your best outfit, muster up your confidence, and watch what you say and how you sit in your chair and what you do with your hands. In other words, they would tell you to put on a little show, a short play that is designed to show your new hypothetical boss just how much of an asset you'd be to his or her company.

Why, then, should you be casual on a first date? If you go through all of this trouble to impress someone who could just give you a job, why wouldn't you put in the same effort—and much, much more—for someone with whom you may end up having a life and having children and growing old together? It makes no sense. As far as we're concerned, romance, in great part, is theatre: we have special costumes we put on and costumes we hope will help transform us into different, more attractive people. We have lines we rehearse in advance—lines we hope will make us seem funny and smart and appealing. And we write little plays in our minds all the time, small dramas starring ourselves—small dramas with great, big happy endings.

Our message, then, is simple. *Act up!* We don't mean, of course, acting up as kids do, throwing tantrums and being difficult. We mean act up like adults, which means unleashing all of your creativity and imagination.

Act up when you're about to go on a first date: consider your dress, your entrance, your timing, and your lines.

But also act up if you've been with your spouse for ages: act up in a way that will help you reinvent yourself and restore the thrill and the romance into your relationship.

As Amy and Dan learned, sometimes all it takes is a tight, red dress and a sexy voice to turn tension into triumph. As Tony and Megan realized, putting on your own show can lead to tremendous intimacy. And as Rebecca and Eric now know, there are moments when pretending to be somebody else can help you breathe new life into a relationship. All these couples incorporated acting into their lives and discovered that, with a little bit of drama, they could make their love more candid, more intimate, and more passionate.

The best part is that acting up is absolutely free. Unlike couples' therapy sessions or romantic cruises or other activities designed to remove you from your everyday environment and put you at ease and encourage you to open up to your spouse, acting up does not cost any money and does not require any advance planning. All you need is a bit of determination and a bit of imagination and you can pull off magic: by pretending to be someone else for a short while, you'll get to better know yourself, better know your partner, and deepen your communication and intimacy.

Let's be clear on one thing: when we tell you to act up, we're not telling you to be phony or insincere or deceitful. We're not telling you to lie or to say anything you don't really mean. It's quite the opposite, actually: what we'll try to help you achieve in this chapter is to learn how to apply a few basic acting techniques to learn how to be yourself more confidently—and improve your love and sex life as you go along. Hey, after all, no one knows about love and sex better than the folks in Hollywood—and Hollywood, as you know by now, is where Stacey Nelkin, the co-author of this book, spent most of her life, acting and dating.

So before we go any further, here's a little acting primer, your own Hollywood guide to love and life:

Know Yourself. Yes, we're saying it again. This may seem a strange thing to say in a chapter about acting. Aren't actors paid to pretend that they're someone else? They are, but the very good ones usually succeed in doing just that precisely by knowing very, very well who they are, so they can look to themselves for ways to identify with the characters they have to play. Before you jump on stage, then, there are some questions you really should answer—questions that will open up your mind and get you in the general mood required to put on a great performance:

Who are you?
This may seem like a weird question, but it really isn't. Try giving a short, honest answer. If you're a little overweight and a little underpaid, but very kind and fiercely loyal to friends and an easygoing, fun person, say so. Don't hide your faults and don't belittle your strengths. You are who you are—and the more intimately you know that person, the better.

How would your friends describe you?
That, of course, is a completely different story. You may see yourself as frugal, for example, while your friends may think you're cheap. Or you may think you're always acting kind of silly, while your friends would say that you're the funniest person they know. Since acting is a social activity and therefore has other people in mind, you can get an excellent idea of what kind of person you are by considering the opinions of your friends.

What have past boyfriends/girlfriends most liked about you?
Now, we're going even deeper—think not only about your friends in general, but about past lovers

in particular. What did they seem to like about you? And what did they dislike?

Know Your Audience. Ask anyone who has ever made a living performing and they'll tell you right away that it's crucial to know your audience. Imagine, for example, how shocked you would be if you went to the movies to see a good romantic comedy and instead were treated to a horror film. Take a good look at your audience—in this case, an audience of one person, your spouse—and ask yourself some key questions:

♦ Is he/she passive or active?
♦ Does he/she prefer passive or active partners?
♦ Is he/she looking to be entertained or does he/she seem to just want some peace and quiet?
♦ In social settings, does he/she light up the dance floor or just slump on the bar?
♦ Does he/she prefer passive or assertive partners?

Once you've ascertained what sort of audience you're working with and what sort of show the audience would like to see, it'll be much easier for you to write, direct, and star in your own little production. It'll be a guaranteed blockbuster.

Looks Matter. Anyone who tells you otherwise is lying. You can be approached by the world's funniest, wittiest, most charming person at a party, but if he or she is fifty pounds overweight, has bad hair and crooked teeth, and is dressed in an old, tattered sweater, the chances are that you'll nod politely and take the first chance you get to move on to some else. It's only natural: we're all human—and we all judge each other and ourselves by our appearances. Here, then, are a few good ideas about looking good:

Pay attention.

Just as no self-respecting actor or actress would ever leave their trailer without making sure their hair, makeup, and clothes are perfect for the scene, neither should you leave your house without making at least a passing effort at looking at your best. Get the best clothes you can afford and the best haircut you can find. Do everything to look your best. How would you know what your best is? It's simple, just …

Own your look.

If you paid attention to the part where we talked about knowing yourself, this should come very easily for you. If not, listen up. Never try to be someone else! If you're short and scrawny with thin arms and thick glasses, the chances are that a really bold shirt wouldn't fit—and if you're a bit chubby, don't even consider those skinny jeans. Instead, find the clothes that work for you—the ones that capture your own sense of style and make you happy and feeling like "you" every time you put them on. If you're still not sure just what those elusive outfits may be, experiment: get a different haircut every now and then and buy at least one item of clothing every few months that you'd never otherwise buy. It's fine to pretend here, too, to act up a little bit—just as long as you try to stay faithful to the things that make you feel comfortable and don't try to force yourself into a totally foreign aesthetic. Sooner or later, you're going to develop a clear, unique style of your own. When you do, make sure that you …

Don't make assumptions.
You know the old saying about how when you assume you make an *ass* out of *u* and *me*? Well, it's true. Don't think, for example, that curvy necessarily means fat: most men, trust us, would rather be with someone who may be a bit round, but who knows and loves her body than with a skinny woman who is insecure about herself and her sexuality—just as most women would take the short, hairy dude who can make them laugh over the tall, tanned, handsome jerk.

It's All About Timing. Are you all dressed up and ready to go? Excellent. But here's another tip that actors learn the hard way: timing is everything. Without it, music doesn't sound good, jokes aren't funny, and flirtations end up badly. So pay attention not only to what you're doing, but also to when you're doing it. If, for example, you put on your sexiest, skimpiest outfit, spray a bit of perfume, and then wrap yourself around your spouse as soon as he or she comes back home from work, and if, say, he or she is clearly distracted because they're still thinking about work or annoyed because they've just been shoved by a rude person on the bus or sad because they've just heard a bit of bad news, no amount of seduction is going to work. Your spouse most likely will see your advances as inappropriate, insensitive, and unappealing. Pay attention to your spouse's body language, to their demeanor, to their tone of voice, and do the right thing at the right time.

Get Into Character. Imagine going to the theatre and seeing the lead actress get up on stage, greet the audience, and then apologize and say she needed a few more minutes before she got into character and could begin acting. Chances are that you'd be furious: you paid to see a show, to get lost in some imagined story. The same goes for your production. Before you act up, make sure you take the time to warm up.

Let's say you decide to imitate Amy and to surprise your spouse by meeting them at some public event, dressed to kill with the attitude to match. Now imagine that before you go to the party, you stop at home, where your spouse is getting ready to go out. You walk through the door, tired and cranky from work. You give your spouse a kiss and go into the bathroom to get ready. No matter what you look and act like when you emerge, the magic is gone: your spouse has already seen you "behind the scenes," and won't be able to imagine you in this brand new role as some fascinating and enigmatic character. Remember that, in relationships, no one wants to go "inside the actors' studio." People want a great performance. So keep things a bit mysterious, a bit out of sight, and make sure that when you see your spouse, you're already in full acting mode.

Once you've gone through all these steps and thought about yourself, your audience, your outfit, your timing and all the other things that go into a great performance, it's time to start acting up. There are, of course, an infinite number of ways you can do it: you can be like

Amy and pull off a bit of performance art to drive your spouse wild. You can be like Tony and Megan and set up your own little theatre production at home, working off somebody else's script. Or you can even be like Rebecca and introduce a bit of explicit, illicit, and mysterious drama into your life. How would you know which is right? Well, if you've thought about yourself and your audience and all the other issues we've just discussed, you'll have no trouble knowing.

Still, acting up is hard to do, so let us help you with a few techniques to get you started on the right foot.

One of the most basic and popular ways to teach acting is to give someone a prop—a toy gun, say—and challenge him or her to come up with scenarios that would involve the object at hand. Try the same at home: grab some prop, whatever catches your eye, sit your partner down on the couch, and try to come up with imaginary scenarios. Some can be real: perhaps you've had some naughty thoughts about the guy who installed your cable or found yourself daydreaming about the checkout girl from the supermarket. Hey, we all fantasize, so why not turn all that sexual energy into a fun little game we can play with our partner? Other prop-related role-playing games can be purely fictional: maybe, for example, you're holding that toy gun because you're a secret spy who's just been caught by the CIA. Or maybe you're a bank robber and your spouse a tough police officer. Sure, these scenarios sound ridiculous, but they're also a lot of fun. Let yourself go and act them out. Get into character. Enjoy. You won't believe how quickly you can get into your role and how sexy things may become if you immerse yourself completely in the drama.

As fun as props are, however, you can't just be improvising all of the time. As any actor will tell you, a solid script is the most important thing there is. Give a great actor bad lines and a dumb plot, and, the chances are that they won't be any good. If you're putting on a show, you'll need a good, strong script.

There are a couple of ways to go about writing a great script. One is to copy Rebecca and come up with a cool, clever plot with which to surprise your partner. Try spending an hour or so—maybe as you commute back home from work, are out walking the dog, or just daydreaming in the shower—about what sort of scenario your partner might find arousing. If he or she is the type for big, bold, sexy surprises, maybe try to replicate Rebecca and send some dirty text messages. If they're a bit more on the gentle side, maybe arrange a more modest adventure such as hiding a few small gifts in key locations around town and then giving your spouse clues and sending her or him on a fun and spirited treasure hunt—the treasure being a hotel room with you in it, smiling and naked.

There are many advantages to going at it alone and surprising your spouse, but it may be even more fun to work on the script together. As Matt Damon and Ben Affleck can tell you, writing scripts together is a blast: how about getting home one night, cracking open a bottle of wine, sitting down at the kitchen table with your spouse and writing one together? It doesn't have to be Oscar material, just something fun to keep you both entertained.

You can try to base the script on your real lives and pretend you're the stars of your own reality show—or invent new characters you'd love to play out. You don't have to write dialogue, of course, but try to get specific with the characters and the plot. Ask questions about their motivation. Get to know them well.

And don't be afraid to make it a sexy movie: for example, one popular and possible script involves both spouses pretending to be other people, stuck in lifeless marriages, and tempted by each other into having an affair. Write the script carefully: do they meet in some out-of-the-way motel? Do they make out in a seedy bar in the sketchy part of town? Do they arrange some secret way to leave each other messages without their spouses finding out? Once you've figured all that out, you have a perfect script to work with. Start acting. Meet at the motel. Go to that bar. Leave those secret messages. Become those cheating lovers. You get to have the forbidden thrill of an affair—only instead of destroying your relationship, it'll actually make it that much stronger and more intimate. You'll be having an affair with your own partner. Now that's dramatic!

Of course, you don't have to go quite that far. Only write something that you're comfortable with and intrigued by, nothing else. Remember that this is a tool— one of the most important ones you'll ever have. Acting serves so many functions: it helps you get comfortable in your own skin, it injects some much-needed variety into your relationships, it puts you and your spouse in strange and interesting new situations, and helps you learn more about each other—plus it's terrific for your sex life and it's completely free.

So go ahead, get on stage, and break a leg.

Five Ways to Act Up Sexy:

Go on a date. One of you speaks and the other listens. For an entire night. Alternate and repeat.

Put on a little play—either one that you've written or one that you like. Make it short. Assign roles: one of you should be the actor and the other the director.

Get home early. Make sure your partner isn't at home. Stand in front of his or her favorite chair. Speak to it as if your partner was there. Tell it everything that's on your mind.

Go to the library or the bookstore. Pick a book you both like. Skim it and find a sexy passage. Act it out.

Come up with a little premise. Go to a crowded, public place. Act it out.

Chapter Three—Shiny, Happy People

Amy hated the Greens. She had met Josh Green in graduate school and thought he was nothing more than a perfectly nice man. Then she met his wife, Caitlin, and took an instant dislike to her. Caitlin was the kind of person who always felt as if they needed to one-up their friends: if you told her your kid learned to read at four, she said hers did at three. If you said you had just bought a new car, she insisted she was about to buy a better one. If you mentioned a book you'd read, she laughed and said she'd read one that was far more intellectual. She was, in short, insufferable.

There was no way, however, that Amy and Dan could turn down Josh and Caitlin's dinner invitation. They'd made up so many excuses over the past few years and were feeling increasingly bad about it. Amy and Josh, after all, worked in the same industry and lived in the same city and knew many of the same people. When she got Josh's e-mail, she wrote and replied that she and Dan would love to attend.

On the short drive over to Josh and Caitlin's house, Amy and Dan rehearsed their plan. They would sit down, have dinner, and then apologize and say the babysitter had to be relieved early and hurry home. They would be polite but make it quick.

It was with this idea in mind that they sat down to dinner. The other two couples, they noticed right away, were quiet and polite, surrendering the conversation to Caitlin. That, however, was not the case with Matt.

He had arrived by himself and was introduced as an old childhood friend of Josh's. Unlike the other men present—all slightly overweight, all wearing faded khaki pants and plain blue button-downs—he was sharply dressed, with beautiful silver cufflinks clasping the sleeves of his crisp white shirt and elegant gray flannel pants falling perfectly straight over strong legs—the kind of legs a man could only have after many hours at the gym.

Best of all, however, was his conversation: he waited politely for Caitlin to stop talking and then regaled the group with short, funny stories, telling them about his kooky, old aunt in Louisiana who was convinced she was a reincarnation of Napoleon, about the time when he got slightly inebriated and managed to convince a roomful of strangers that he was an important British author, and about his epic trip to Venice to see great art.

Venice! Amy had always dreamed of going there, but somehow had always put it off, and now they had kids and jobs and the economy being what it is and here, she thought, was this stranger, this handsome, eloquent man, telling stories about watching the sunset over the canals and looking at paintings in ancient cathedrals and eating perfect meals at tiny restaurants.

As much as she tried to hide it, Amy was blushing. She wasn't used to men like Matt, so charming and at ease.

She loved Dan very much, but he, like most of the men she knew, was frumpy and clueless, the kind of guy who would watch eight hours of sports with great pleasure, but who considered ten minutes of shopping for clothes to be cruel and unusual punishment. Once, before the kids were born, Amy had tried to convince Dan to splurge on a romantic vacation in Italy; he laughed and said that Epcot would be better—they would pay less money and get to visit more countries. He was kindhearted and caring but in no way the kind of man you'd see in old, romantic movies.

Matt, however, was, and after dinner was over and the party had moved to the living room, Amy found herself ignoring the plans she had made earlier—the plans calling for an immediate retreat as soon as the meal was over—and instead made her way to the white leather couch, where she sat next to Matt and struck up a conversation.

To her delight, he was even more terrific one-on-one than he was addressing the entire group. He asked her clever and insightful questions about her work, knew all of her favorite painters and composers well, and regaled her with more stories of his travels. Dan, she could see out of the corner of her eye, was talking baseball with Rob, a burly, bearded man. Surely, she thought, he wouldn't mind if she spent some time chatting up this lovely and intelligent man.

Only Dan did mind. An hour later, well after the time they had planned to leave, he walked silently to the car. He didn't say a word as they drove back home. He remained quiet as they got ready for bed.

"What's going on?" she finally asked him. "Why the silent treatment?"

With that, Dan erupted. Hissing his words through his teeth, he accused her of flirting with Matt, of coming on to him, of embarrassing Dan in front of their friends.

Amy was shocked; she realized, of course, that she was attracted to the handsome stranger she had just met, but didn't think she had behaved in any inappropriate way. Why was Dan so jealous? And was he right? Had she been unfaithful? No, she told herself again, that's crazy: she had done nothing wrong.

Exhausted from arguing with her husband, Amy ducked under the covers and pretended to be asleep. Then, however, she sat up in bed and, doing her best to stay calm, began to speak. She didn't plan the speech and didn't know what she was going to say before she said it. She opened her mouth and told her husband the truth.

She liked Matt's shirt and the way he waited for a few moments after every sentence—just to make sure everyone around the table was following him. She liked the fact that he was interested in art and that he was well traveled. And yes, she found him attractive. But not, she said as softly as she could, as attractive as Dan.

"You," she told her husband, "are the man I love—and even if I spend all night talking to a charming stranger who wears silver cufflinks and has been to Venice, you're the only man I want to go to bed with every night."

Dan smiled. "Oh, yeah?" he asked.

"Oh, yeah," Amy replied.

"Why don't you come here and prove it?" said Dan. It was all the invitation Amy needed: she rolled over and kissed her husband passionately. He kissed her back—

kissed her and caressed her with a sort of vitality she hadn't felt from him in a long time. When they were done making love, Amy turned to her husband and, in a sultry voice, told him it was the best sex she'd ever had. She hesitated for a minute and then looked her husband right in the eye.

"I guess I should talk to handsome men at parties more often," she said, "if that's what it takes to get you so wild."

To her relief, Dan laughed. "Don't push your luck, lady," he said, and lunged at her. Soon, they were kissing again, and, again, made love. It was a very good night.

*   *   *

It was freezing cold that morning. Megan, popping into the Starbucks near her office on the way to work, was especially eager to get a hot drink in her hands. As she put her hands on the cold, metal handle of the door, she saw him immediately through the glass. He was a new barista and, as he fumbled with the register, she was struck by how good-looking he was. He was young, confident, and charming. He had the same easygoing manner that had attracted her to Tony. After casually placing her order, she walked over to the far line to wait for her latte. She innocently glanced over in his direction. Her eyes met his and he smiled, she was pleased to think, for a bit longer than he should have. She felt an instant tingle, and, for that brief moment, she felt sexy—an object of desire and mystery. His name, she learned from the tag on his shirt, was Sean. He wore a tight gray t-shirt and had light blond stubble on his cheeks.

As she sat through one boring meeting after another that morning, her thoughts often drifted to Sean. She never had more than one cup of java a day—it gave her the shakes—but that afternoon, she walked into the same Starbucks and bought herself an espresso. It was bitter and made her stomach turn, but it was worth it just to see him again, to see that gorgeous smile and tousled hair.

There was something new, unexplored, and exciting about Sean. Megan was giddy. Soon enough, however, the guilt started creeping in. She sighed when she thought of Tony and their dinner plans for that night.

It wasn't that she didn't love Tony: she was still very much certain that he was the love of her life and was very happy to be married to him. But something in their love life had recently begun to die down. With all the pressures of him losing his job, with the economy crashing down all around them, they found their sex life in a slump, a little repetitive and nowhere near as thrilling and frequent as it had been when they were first married. Megan was bored—and, deep down, Tony was, too.

Or at least she thought he was. He wasn't the kind to share his feelings with others, but there was definitely a change taking over him. While he once had a huge appetite for sex—sometimes suggesting lovemaking several times a day—now he mostly jumped into bed, muttered a few words about being beat or depressed, and drifted right to sleep. Often, Megan couldn't help but feel that he was just looking for an excuse to not sleep with her. And, deep inside, she couldn't blame him: she, too, was feeling overwhelmed, being the family's sole breadwinner, and she, too, only wanted to put on her nightgown, jump into bed, and go to sleep. She thought about all of this on her way to dinner and it made her sad.

A few words were exchanged that night at their favorite little restaurant. Tony was lost in his thoughts and Megan, for her part, wondered what Sean was doing at that very moment. Probably out with his friends, she imagined, having fun, flirting. Just as she used to, she thought, when she was young.

As the weeks passed, Sean became a bigger and bigger part of Megan's life. At first, she just smiled at him, grabbed her drink, and quickly exited the store—afraid that if she lingered for another moment, she wouldn't be able to control herself. But Sean was very sweet, and, gradually, he made Megan feel comfortable. He memorized her regular order, for example, and handed it to her with a few warm words. He complimented her on a pair of earrings she especially liked. When she spent a few days in Miami for a work-related conference, he commented on her tan, telling her how much it suited her.

She grew easy around Sean, happily chatted with him, eager to learn as much about him as she could. She also noticed another, subtle change: she now took more time to get ready in the mornings, spending another half hour in front of the mirror, choosing her outfits more carefully. The more she was aware of her behavior, the more uncomfortable she felt: there was no denying it— she was openly, clearly, unashamedly flirting with Sean.

And then, one day, everything came crashing down. It was Monday morning, and Tony, who had a job interview a few blocks down from Megan's office, suggested they ride the subway together. As they emerged back onto the street, Megan said she'd like to go to Starbucks to grab a coffee. To her horror, Tony, who rarely had coffee in the mornings, said he'd like one, too. There was little she could say or do. She walked into the store and watched with horror as her young, handsome barista smiled at her, handed her her coffee before she even had a chance to order it, and asked her about a film she had told him she intended to watch over the weekend.

Out of the corner of her eye, she caught a glimpse of Tony. He looked stunned and hurt. Megan felt terrible. He paid for both of their drinks and they left in silence— not saying anything to each other.

That evening, they had dinner in silence. Finally, Tony said something and Megan replied—before they knew it, they were bickering. Then, before she realized what had hit her, Tony let it out: "I'm sorry," he said bitterly, "that I can't be as cool as your friend at the coffee shop."

Megan had no idea what to say. On the one hand, she knew full well that she was guilty of flirting with Sean. But was that really wrong? She hadn't, after all, done anything bad, hadn't cheated on Tony, and hadn't betrayed his trust. All she did was be nice to a barista. Okay, maybe a little bit too nice, but still. She was confused.

"Maybe you can be," she said, surprised to hear her voice take on a playful, kittenish tone. "Maybe if you mess up your hair just so." With that, she leaned in toward her husband and ran her fingers through his hair.

Tony froze for a few moments, but then let out a little smile. "Oh, yeah?" he said, relaxing his tense shoulders. "So maybe I should also unbutton my shirt a little—just like him." And so he did. After a few more minutes of banter, Megan and Tony were on the kitchen floor, making love passionately. Whenever Megan thought of

Sean after that night, it was no longer as a mysterious fantasy stranger, but as the man who helped her and her husband jumpstart their sex life. A little flirting was all they needed to rekindle their marriage.

*   *   *

If they stayed at home, Rebecca and Eric knew, they'd get no work done. And even though it was a Sunday, there was plenty they had to do. Eric had promised his boss a ten-page report on the company's newest product by Monday morning and he wasn't even halfway done. Rebecca had been asked to give a speech at her best friend's upcoming wedding—a speech she dreaded and needed to write down word-for-word if she wasn't to mess it up. To minimize distractions, they decided to camp out at a nearby coffee shop and work until they were both done.

With steaming cappuccinos at hand, they grabbed a corner table, took out their laptop computers, and started writing. No more than an hour later, however, they were both bored—or at least Eric was. The report seemed interminable, and there were only so many things he had to say. He hit "save," took a long sip of the now-cold coffee, and looked around.

His gaze immediately wandered to a table at the other end of the café, where three young women, roughly his age, sat and talked. They looked, he thought, like something out of a movie. One was a tanned blonde with a pink cardigan and large golden earrings, one a brunette in a sharply tailored dress, and the third a redhead in jeans and a T-shirt. *Straight out of central casting,* Eric thought, giggling silently to himself.

Or so he thought. A moment later, catching Rebecca's quizzical look, he realized that he hadn't been successful at keeping his thoughts to himself.

"What's out of central casting?" Rebecca asked, smiling.

"Nothing," Eric replied. "I can't believe I said that out loud."

Still, he was unable to look away from the trio of gorgeous girls, and soon Rebecca was staring at them, too. Eric was horrified: here he was, caught red-handed, and Rebecca would probably soon give him a piece of her mind. He sighed softly, expecting a speech about what a jerk he was for checking out other girls, about how this behavior was insulting and concerning, about how she could no longer be sure if he truly loved her or was constantly looking for someone else—someone more attractive—to come along. To his surprise, Rebecca said something very different.

"Which one would you do?" she asked.

Eric was shocked. Had he misheard?

"Sorry?" he mumbled, but Rebecca was unfazed. "Come on," she said, "you were totally checking them out. Which one of them would you most like to have sex with—if you could?"

"No one!" Eric answered quickly. "I only want to go home with you!"

Rebecca laughed. "You're sweet," she said, "but we're talking fantasy here. Theoretically, if you had no girlfriend and were available and were sitting here by yourself looking at these three fine ladies—which one would you most like to take home?"

Eric was enjoying this. Rebecca never ceased to amaze him. He decided to play along.

"You know what?" he asked. "Let's make this a bit more interesting. Which one do you think I'd pick?"

Rebecca squealed with joy. "Fun game!" she shrieked. Then, she studied the three women, pretending to be a scholar looking at a strange specimen. "Hmmm," she said, "let's see. The brunette is too preppy for you, so she's out. It's between Little Miss Blonde Sorority here and Wild Child Red. You know what? I say the redhead. Am I right?"

Eric beamed. "Bravo!" he said. "Yes, yes you are. She's hot."

"She is," Rebecca said, without a trace of jealousy. Suddenly, she got up and Eric watched with amazement as she walked across the room, approached the three women, and struck up a conversation. He couldn't hear what they were talking about, but a moment later all four of them were headed his way. Smiling, Rebecca introduced him to her new acquaintances, and said she'd invited the trio over to join her and Eric to save the both of them from a boring afternoon filled with chores.

For a few minutes, Eric just sat there, having little to say as Rebecca and her new friends chatted about this and that. Soon, however, he came back to his senses and dove right into the conversation. The women, he learned, were all nurses at a nearby hospital and were enjoying some time off before a night shift. They were a lot of fun, he thought. He also didn't miss Rebecca's efforts to give the redheaded nurse—whose name was Trish—special attention.

An hour later, the nurses had to go and the group exchanged e-mail addresses. After they had said their goodbyes, Rebecca playfully handed Eric a piece of paper.

"Here," she said. "Trish's address. Will you e-mail her?"

"No," Eric said, smiling coyly and sliding the paper back into Rebecca's hand. "But I will e-mail you, devil woman." He put his hand on her thigh.

"Come on," she said. "Let's go home. I think we need to be alone."

*   *   *

If you paid any attention to the subtitle of this book, you know that we promised you all that you need to save your relationship is an empty wallet and a dirty mind. We've spent some time talking about the former; it's time to touch on the latter.

Before we even begin, however, let us get one thing straight: we all have dirty minds. Even the most polite among us—those who regularly attend church or synagogue or mosque and who are kind to the elderly and helpful to their colleagues and saintly to their neighbors—sometimes find themselves entertaining some filthy little thought, some raunchy fantasy, or some X-rated daydream. Hallelujah to that! Imagine how boring and sterile our lives would be without the occasional thrill of allowing ourselves to be swept into a steamy, sexy reverie.

But the mind, let us not forget, is a muscle, and like every other muscle, it needs exercise. This is especially true in the case of thinking about sex: the more you think about it—the more aroused and imaginative you become—the more likely you are to improve your actual sex life. This chapter is all about exercising that muscle—take it from us, it's the best exercise you'll ever have.

In the book's first two chapters, we focused on getting to know yourself and your partner and on being creative, communicative, and candid. However, no relationship—as Dan and Amy, Megan and Tony, and Rebecca and Eric learned all too well—is airtight. Even if you follow our advice and create a sexy, supportive environment for you and your partner, soon enough you're going to discover, as our three couples did, that there are other people all around you and that they affect the way you see yourself and your partner. They can have an immense impact on what you naively thought was just a relationship between you and your spouse.

Put simply, what our three couples have learned is this: people flirt. It's inevitable. It happens to everyone—even the most faithful and loyal and responsible among us. Why? Our dirty minds may have something to do with it: as long as we're alive, we're sexual beings, and as long as that's the case, we're going to seek—however mildly—the attention and attraction of people we find appealing.

This, of course, doesn't mean that flirtation is akin to infidelity or that we flirt with strangers because we're unhappy in our own relationship. We do it for a variety of other reasons. Here are some of them:

♦ **It feels good**. We don't care who you are or what kind of relationship you're in, smiling at someone—and having someone smile at you—feels really good. It doesn't have to go anywhere. It doesn't have to mean anything. But whatever it is, it's always fun.

♦ **It takes you back**. Remember the days when you were young and unattached and every stranger you saw was a potential partner and flirting was the first and necessary step en route to relationship. You should—and flirting helps jog your memory.

♦ **It makes you feel desired**. Like it or not, if you spend enough time with one person, eventually there will be very little new or exciting about them. Flirting with other people tells you that you're still attractive, still sexy, still someone that other people may consider as a potential partner.

♦ **It teaches you things**. You'll learn things about yourself, things about your partner, things that may not have otherwise come to the surface.

♦ **It shakes things up**. As much as we all enjoy the safety and stability of marriage, there's something to be said about a little bit of friendly competition every now and then. Your partner may not really think they will lose you for someone else, but seeing you smile at someone—or dance with someone at a party—may push him or her to put their game faces on, get in there and try hard—maybe harder than they have in a very long time—to reassert their love and passion for you and vice versa.

Convinced? Great. There's still, however, the matter of caution. Let us be very clear about this: we are not advocating being unfaithful, nor do we think you should flirt with other people to make your partner jealous. And, of course, we think that you should have a little talk with your partner to decide what your mutual boundaries are and to make sure you're both on the same page. The only thing we are suggesting is to acknowledge that flirting goes on all around us and to learn how to use it to our advantage, to make us feel better, and to spice up our relationships. It's one of these tricks that requires very little investment and yields giant rewards, and, particularly in this economic climate, we all love those.

Think of flirting, then, as a space heater. Keeping it on for the right amount of time and keeping it at a safe distance will make everything nice and hot. However, if you neglect the basic safety rules, things may catch on fire and burn down your house. To help keep things cool, to know how to translate the immense benefits of flirting into positive sexual and relationship energy, and to summarize everything we've just talked about, we've come up with a set of guidelines. It's very basic stuff—but it's crucial. Here goes:

♦ **There's no right or wrong when it comes to flirting**. Really, it's all about figuring out what works for you and your partner. Some people, such as Rebecca, would like to go very far, and others, such as Tony, prefer to keep things at a safe distance. You know yourself and you know your partner, so you should have no problem figuring out some form of flirting that would work well for both of you.

♦ **The rules are everything**. Flirting, after all, is a game—and the first thing a game needs are clear rules. Make sure you know what they are and make sure you play nice. Otherwise, feelings get hurt and relationships get ruined.

♦ **The rules can change**. Having rules doesn't mean the same rules apply in every situation and at every time. People go through phases—and moods and circumstances change. Make sure you and your partner update your rulebook as often as necessary.

♦ **It's about playing**. Sure, it's hard to look at your significant other—a person with whom you've shared so much in life—as a mere toy, but flirting gives you just that type of fun and frivolous energy.

♦ **It's the take-away of relationships**. It's the same as getting food somewhere outside the house and then bringing it in and sharing it with your partner. Don't eat it by yourself—and don't forget that the bottom line is to make the relationship better.

We hope that we are able to convince you to set your imagination free, to learn that it's okay to think about other people in a sexual way, and to translate these fantasies and flirtations into raw sexual energy that you can use in your own bedroom with your partner. However, as so many other things else in life, flirting, too, is really a hands-on type of thing; we can talk about it all we want, but until you try it, you'll never know just how thrilling, how rewarding, and how enriching it can be. So, to help you out, here's a little something to get you started:

To Flirt Or Not To Flirt?

Here's a fun little quiz; take it alone or with a partner, use it to get some ideas for flirting or to ask questions about acceptable boundaries. Tally up your score and see where you stand.

1. **Let's be honest about it: when it comes to flirting, I'm:**
    a. A lost cause. I can't pull it off. It's just too weird or too awkward.
    b. One of the gang. I'm no expert on the stuff, but some witty banter and some sexual tension with strangers every now and then is nice.
    c. The master. No one is better at playing a room, and it makes me feel very sexy.
2. **When I think about it, my definition of flirting is:**
    a. Anything that is not pleasant and professional conduct, thank you very much!
    b. That spark between two people, that smile, that inviting body gesture. Trust me, I'll know it when I see it.
    c. Everything! Almost every interaction between two people can be a flirt waiting to break free.
3. **I'm at a party with my partner, when suddenly he/ she strikes up a conversation with a very attractive member of the opposite sex. It's all harmless stuff, really, but I can't help but notice that my partner**

is being a little too smooth and that the gorgeous stranger is doing the same. I:

a. Insert myself between these two, say a few terse words, and drag my partner away. Has he/she no shame?

b. Do nothing. Who cares who my partner is talking to?

c. Smile happily. It turns me on to see my partner as the object of someone else's desire and to know that I'm the one who gets to take him/her home with me.

4. I only consider it flirting if:

a. My significant other isn't there. Flirting in front of my partner is rude.

b. My significant other isn't there. Or is there. Either way, it's flirting when I feel like it's flirting.

c. My significant other is there. After all, what's the point of flirting if my partner isn't there to watch and to get a kick out of it?

5. When my partner is around, it's perfectly fine for me to flirt with someone:

a. Never. It's simply unacceptable.

b. For a little while, say, a few minutes at most. Anything more than that and it becomes uncomfortable.

c. For as long as I want! Why be cruel and put a cap on flirting?

6. I know, I know, I'm a flirt. But why do I do it?

a. Revenge, of course. My partner is a flirt and I feel compelled to play the game.

b. Relationship currency, I guess. I want my spouse to know that others still consider me sexy and that if he/she wants to keep me, they better work hard at it.

   c. Duh—I do it because it's fun!

7. **I'm at a restaurant, and my partner has been flirting shamelessly with the waiter/waitress. I've been noticing it all evening! In response, I:**

   a. Get up, slap my partner for being so demeaning and unfaithful, make a little scene, and run out of the restaurant.

   b. Just watch. I don't care. Or maybe I'm kind of getting off on watching this scene. Either way, I won't let it interrupt my meal.

   c. Find my own waiter/waitress and immediately begin flirting with them. Hey, two can play that game!

8. **My partner and I are standing in line for the movies when the person behind us in line strikes up a conversation with my partner. Pretty soon, it's all giggles and banter. I just know that I:**

   a. Wouldn't be able to control myself and would just grab that rude person and beat them up. How dare they?

   b. Shoot the stranger dirty looks but do nothing else of significance.

   c. Join in the fun conversation!

9. **I'm at the gym, all sweaty and gross, when this hot gym-goer with an amazing body starts chatting me up. I:**

   a. Feel very uncomfortable. That person's hot and all, but I'm with someone else.

   b. Don't read too much into it. It's just a little friendly chitchat.

    c. Can't wait until I get home and tell my partner all about it as we're tearing the clothes off each other's backs.

10. By far, the thing I love most about flirting is:

    a. Nothing. The whole thing is just awkward and uncomfortable.

    b. The way it makes me feel. So wanted, so sexy.

    c. Thinking about how I can take this sexy feeling and bring it home to my partner.

Results:

Here's how to rate yourself on this quiz: give yourself 3 points for each time you've answered A, 5 points for each time you've answered B, and 10 points for each time you've answered C. Tally up the points. If you got:

Less than 40 points: Oh my. The very thought of smiling at a stranger or striking up a conversation with someone you don't know strikes you as a cardinal sin. Life should be about fun, my friend, not fear. You may want to reread this chapter and think again about how you and your partner see your relationship.

Between 50 and 70 points: Sometimes you'll flirt and when you do, you admit it. Still, you find the whole concept weird—something that no one in a relationship should really do. Lighten up a bit and life will smile at you.

Between 70 and 80 points: When you were born, you probably winked at the doctor flirtatiously. Otherwise, it's hard to explain how comfortable you feel in this territory. Take this amazing energy and use it for the best.

Between 80 and 100 points: Clear the bars, shut down the parties, and lock up the towns. You're on the loose and you'll flirt with anyone and everyone. We're happy to see you so confident, but remember to be careful. Some people may take your attitude the wrong way.

Five Sexy Musts:

Sex is play: go to your local store and get some adult toys.

Food is sexy: an ice cube in the right place—or some chocolate in the nude—could go a long way toward making things steamier.

Location, location, location: forget about the bedroom and try to find new and exciting places to do it—in your home or outside of it.

If you stay in bed, however, at least make sure you have nice, soft, sensuous, sexy sheets. It makes a world of a difference.

There is more than one position of lovemaking. Try each one you know at least once—and then spend some time thinking up new ones.

Chapter Four—Can't Buy Me Love

Dan and Amy sat on their living room floor, surrounded by a sea of papers and hills of brown cardboard boxes. It was after ten o'clock and the kids had just gone to bed. Although they were both tired after a long day of work, they knew the task ahead had to be done: Tax Day was fast approaching and they had to go through their bills and sort out their finances.

As Amy made a good portion of her money taking on freelance projects here and there, taxes were a convoluted affair for the couple and demanded long hours of going over every receipt, every bill, and every bit of income and expense. They were both bad with numbers and put it off for as long as they could. Yet, here it was, all their bills and bank statements scattered on the floor, waiting to suck them in.

They had tried, of course, to make tax night—that's what they had taken to calling it a few years back—as fun as possible, promising each other that as soon as the calculations were done, they'd reward themselves with a nice bubble bath or a lovely bottle of wine. But as soon as they began looking at the long, threatening lines, punching numbers into their small calculator and filling up page after page with scribbled calculations, they grew quiet with anxiety. It had been a very bad year.

As it had most people, the spiraling economy had hurt them: Dan was informed that he would not get the raise he was promised long ago, a bit of news that actually made him happy—it meant, he thought, that he wasn't getting fired, at least not for now. Amy, who once could count on a nice annual sum to flow in from her side projects, barely had any clients at all, and the few she had received a far discounted rate to encourage them to continue to give her business. Yet, here they were, owing taxes even on the puny sum she had managed to earn. She was sad and frustrated. She said the first thing that came to her mind.

"I swear," she muttered. "I should've been a prostitute."

Dan froze and looked at her. The expression on his face was strange—a combination of curiosity and disgust.

"Don't look at me like that," she said, smiling. "You know how much money we would've made if I was a hooker? These girls turn in two grand a night—all under the table. And there's no way that their clients are nastier than some of the guys I have to deal with in my job."

"Stop," Dan said tersely. But he was smiling. Amy decided to keep on playing her silly game.

"I'm telling you," she said, "we should seriously consider it. You can be my business manager."

"If I was your business manager," he said, inching closer toward her, "I'd spend all of our money paying you so I could be your only client."

"Paying me for sex, eh?" Amy felt herself getting turned on by the conversation. "How could you afford it without your raise? I'm not cheap, you know."

"I'll find a way," Dan said, looking at his wife mischievously. "You know I'm very crafty when there's something I really want."

"I'm glad I found a way to motivate you," she said, kissing his neck. "The taxes can wait; let's give my hypothetical new career a break and make old-fashioned love, shall we?"

And they did—with passion—several times that evening. Tax night, they agreed, had never been quite so fun.

*   *   *

Megan was the only one of her friends not looking forward to the birthday party. When she and her girlfriends were younger, birthdays meant long nights out on the town, fruity drinks spiked with vodka or rum, and silly but sweet gifts such as over-the-top sexy lingerie or a chocolate-making workshop at a local store. Never a big lover of birthdays—who, she thought, needed to be reminded that she was getting older?—Megan still enjoyed these celebrations with her friends and covered the big bulletin board in her office with snapshots taken over the years: here she was with her friends at Marissa's twenty-eighth birthday party, the lot of them drunk on a cheesy booze cruise, and here they were again, a few years later, celebrating Joanna's thirtieth at a cheap Spanish restaurant downtown. These, she often thought, were magical moments.

But recently, she noticed, birthdays came to mean something completely different. As soon as her friends started having children—and by now, most of them had had at least one baby—birthdays became less about them and more about the kids. Instead of celebrating Marissa's birthday, for example, she'd be invited to celebrate with Torrie, Marissa's toddler, and instead of sipping sangria with Joanna, she drank apple juice at the birthday party of Teddy, her three-year-old son. So when Janie invited her to yet another afternoon filled with cake and juice and children with sticky fingers, Megan shot Tony a sad look and pleaded for him to come along.

They were sitting on Janie's couch, a gaggle of children running and screaming happily all around them. Naturally, the conversation turned to the economic situation.

It was the sort of chat that seemed almost unavoidable nowadays among Megan and Tony's set of friends: each person in his or her turn would share horror stories of layoffs and cutbacks and then speak longingly about the good ol' days, just a few years back, when their mutual funds still had enough cash to allow them to retire at a decent age and their bank accounts had enough spare change to pay for a nice vacation here and there. And since this was a children's party, the cost of raising children came up and one couple after the other moaned about everything from the cost of private schools to how difficult it had suddenly become to pay for a good nanny.

Having no children to look after, Megan had emptied a few glasses of chardonnay, and with her mind clouded by the wine, joined in on the conversation. "I'm sorry if

I sound like a bitch," she said, "but listening to all of you talk, I'm really glad Tony and I don't have any kids. You know, with Tony being laid off and all, and with living off my salary alone, we barely make it through the month. I can't even begin to imagine what we would have done if we had another mouth or two to feed."

Her friends all nodded in sympathy and soon the conversation moved on. But Tony, she could see, had not: he was sitting next to her and as soon as she finished speaking, jerked his entire body in the opposite direction, as if trying his best to avoid touching her. She wondered why he was angry. She didn't have to wait long to find out.

"I can't believe you said what you said," he said as soon as they left their friends' apartment.

"What did I say?" Megan asked, confused.

"Don't play dumb," Tony hissed at her. "You know damn well what you said."

Megan was taken aback. She had never heard Tony speak to her in that way before and had never heard him sound so cruel and unkind. She wasn't sure what she should say. Why, she thought, was he so upset? What had she said? All she could recall was telling their friends that things were a bit rough financially—could that be why Tony was mad? It made no sense to her.

"Tony," she said, trying hard not to cry, "I don't know what I said. And I'm sorry if I offended you. Please tell me why you're so mad."

Tony stopped walking and turned around sharply to face her. There were tears in his eyes, angry tears. "I'm mad because you just humiliated me in front of all of our friends," he shouted at her. "You made me seem like a huge loser who couldn't even afford to have kids. Are you happy with the way things are, Megan? Are you happy to be the only one who has a job? Does it make you feel all powerful? Just do me a favor and don't take it out on me."

Megan stood, listening and sobbing quietly. How, she thought, could Tony think that she wished this on him? How could he possibly think she was enjoying being the sole breadwinner in the family? And why on earth did he take her innocent comment as a personal attack? She'd never called him a loser and never said he was too poor to have kids. All she did was be honest. She searched for something to say, but since no words came to mind, she stood crying in the middle of the street. Tony was now rapidly walking away and Megan followed a step or two behind, not wanting to have anything to do with him. When they got to their apartment, he stormed into the bedroom and she threw herself on the living room couch. They spent the rest of the afternoon in silence.

As they were getting ready for bed that night, however, Megan felt a seething rage flood her stomach. She had been replaying Tony's harsh words in her mind for hours and the more she thought about it, the more she became increasingly incensed. She stormed into the bathroom, where Tony was brushing his teeth.

"You owe me an apology," she said sternly.

"I'm sorry," Tony said meekly. "I was just a bit freaked out that you shared all of this intimate stuff with all those people. It made it seem like I, you know, like I wasn't a good husband. Like I couldn't satisfy you."

"Can you?" Megan asked. Tony looked at her, confused.

"I mean," she said, "right now. Can you satisfy me right now?"

Still, Tony stood there, staring at her, not moving.

"Come on!" she said, letting all of her anger burst out. "Take me to bed and satisfy me. Or are you unemployed in the bedroom also?"

"Megan!" Tony cried out his wife's name. Why, he thought, was she saying those things? Was she trying to hurt him back? Whatever it was, she wouldn't stop.

"Come on!" she was now shouting. "What's the matter? Can't make love to your wife without that big fat bonus you're used to getting every year? Can't have sex without your long and hard corporate title? Wanna prove you're not a loser? Take me to bed. Now."

Something clicked in Tony. He stopped hearing, stopped seeing, and stopped being confused. The only thing he noticed now was how quickly his own heart was beating—how aroused he was to hear his wife talk that way. She was calling into question his self-worth as a man and his every muscle ached to prove her wrong. With a bit more force than he was used to, he grabbed her arm and dragged her into the bedroom. He threw her on the bed and made love to her for a long, long time. They fell asleep that night in each other's arms, exhausted, but reconciled and very much in love.

*   *   *

"How the hell did you get promoted?"

Eric was happy for Rebecca, but he found the news that she had to tell him a bit overwhelming: her company, it seemed, had merged two of its divisions because of the recession and needed a seasoned person to manage the new, extended staff. Therefore, in the middle of the hardest of times, Rebecca was called into her boss's office, offered a new title, and given an enormous raise. She was telling him all this on the phone, squealing with excitement.

"What can I tell ya?" she said, laughing. "Some gals just get all the luck."

"We have to celebrate," Eric said. "Absolute must. How about I take you out for a nice dinner tonight?"

Rebecca snorted. "Babe," she said in a low, sexy voice, "I'm the one swimming in it, remember? *I'm* taking *you* out tonight. I'll have my assistant—can you believe I have an assistant now?—I'll ask her to make us good reservations. So wear something pretty, eh?"

Eric recognized her tone right away. It was the same playful macho tone he often took when he was trying to act all manly and casual—the tone that men such as Humphrey Bogart perfected in all of his favorite classic movies. But coming from Rebecca—a woman—it somehow sounded different, more exotic, more arousing. It was as if she was the cool, nonchalant hero and he was the swooning damsel. He couldn't wait for the evening.

After work, Eric ran home and changed into his most attractive outfit. He stopped by a local florist and picked up a single red rose. Then, he rushed to the restaurant; he was ready to woo his girl.

As soon as he walked in, however, he knew that it would be Rebecca who would be doing the wooing: she was leaning against the bar, dressed in a gorgeous, flowing black dress, her hair falling over her shoulders, a champagne flute in her hand. When she saw Eric, she smiled a little smile and motioned with her finger for him to approach. He walked over; she grabbed the back of his head and brought him in closer for a kiss.

"Hey, gorgeous," she said. He gulped. It was his favorite line—the thing he said to her every time they met. "I got you this," he said, handing her the red rose. She thanked him with a kiss and then pulled a small package from her purse. "And I got you this," she said, handing it to him. "Go ahead, open it."

Eric did and let out a little yelp when he saw what was inside: it was a rare first edition of his favorite book from childhood—a collectors' item, he knew—that must have cost Rebecca a few hundred dollars.

"I know you've always wanted this," she said sweetly. "And now I can afford it. I hope you like it."

Eric told her he did, very much, and kissed her again. They sat down at their table and Rebecca ordered the expensive, elaborate tasting menu for them both. Eric felt lightheaded. It wasn't, he knew, just the wine he'd been drinking: he was accustomed to spending lavishly on his girlfriends and very much enjoyed these grand romantic gestures such as buying thoughtful gifts or treating to luxurious meals. Yet here was Rebecca doing all of this for him—and it felt both strange and wonderful. He was enjoying the attention, but it was hard to get over the fact that he wasn't—wasn't what?—he couldn't even put it into words. It was just, he finally thought, that with Rebecca buying him gifts and taking him out to dinner, he wasn't feeling like much of a man.

He thought about this in the cab on their way over to Rebecca's place. He wondered if she would be any different in the bedroom now that she seemed to be enjoying her newfound status. But she surprised him.

"I love you," she whispered softly when they finally got into bed. "Let's make love."

After spending an entire evening acting cool and enjoying the attention, Eric realized, Rebecca was now ready to let him shine, wanted him to make love to her as he had before. He realized that she was telling him that although she now made much more money than he did and although she enjoyed playing it up from time to time, nothing would ever change the foundation of their relationship.

Eric held Rebecca tight and kissed her wildly. He had never felt like more of a man before.

*   *   *

Growing up, the chances are good that your mother told you there were some topics one just didn't talk about in polite company: politics, religion, sex, and, most likely, money. This last one is particularly baffling to us: we know people who would share the most intimate details of their sex lives with their closest friends, yet would never share the most basic information about their finances—such as how much they made each year or how much they managed to put aside in savings. Somehow, many people still seem to think that talking about money—even with their partners—is simply bad manners.

We're not going to be so well behaved. Talking about money, we firmly believe, is one of the most awkward—yet most important things—that you can do in a relationship. If you don't believe us, just read any survey listing popular causes for divorce and each one will tell you the same thing—most divorced couples are motivated, at least in part, by some issue or another related to money. More often than not, it's not being poor that brings people to divorce court, but rather some strange, inexplicable inability to be candid about cash before or during their marriage.

Before we go any further, then, here are the fundamentals of how to safely and productively introduce money talk into your relationship:

♦ **Be Open**. You could've seen that one coming, couldn't you? Yet there is no more important piece of advice that we can give. Day after day, in both our personal and professional lives, we see people who broke this rule and paid dearly for it: husbands who hid their bad credit and wives who secretly ran through their savings—a whole gallery of shame and regret. More often than not, keeping financial secrets leads to a rude awakening and other minor catastrophes. So take this simple advice and just be honest.

♦ **Know Your Money Matters**. We don't mean just having a basic understanding of how a mutual fund works—although that's easy enough to do nowadays and well worth the effort—but rather knowing just what it is that you'd like to have money for. This is no silly question: some of us get off on saving for a rainy day, while others believe that life is short and spending money makes it better. You and your spouse should have a long, philosophical talk to realize just how each of you sees money and its uses.

♦ **Keep an Eye Open**. While some things in life stay the same—your sense of humor, your taste in clothes—others, money among them, change all the time. Incomes rise and fall, expenses shrink and mushroom, and the market constantly fluctuates. Just as you keep on top of your favorite sports team or you know a little bit about the newest fashion out of Milan, make it a habit to follow up on your finances—and make sure that all is as it should be.

♦ **Money's Blind**. It doesn't see any traditional roles. Don't go by the old and archaic gender roles, deciding that the man should have most responsibilities and the woman should have little—if any. Instead, go with what feels comfortable and natural, consider your respective incomes, your likes and dislikes, and try to build a financial partnership that makes sense in your particular situation.

♦ **The Hard Questions Are the Only Ones That Matter**. Sooner or later, you're going to come across some major questions—questions that may involve huge risks and large expenditures and may have a great impact on your lives and your future. Talk about them! This may sound obvious, but you'll be surprised to learn how many couples prefer to put off heavy, mirthless discussions about somber things such as wills or emergency funds. Talk about everything and try to have a plan for every possible disaster. As the old scouting motto goes, be prepared.

This may seem like obvious stuff—and, in many ways, it is. Don't knock it down, though. If the obvious was so obvious indeed, we wouldn't all be making the same mistakes, right? However, we'd like to take things another step further. Even more important than learning how to talk about money in a safe and successful manner is learning how to talk about money in a sexy way.

Don't worry, we're not going to be like those pesky pundits on television who suggest you try—as Dan and Amy did—to make an evening of poring over tax returns fun by sharing a bottle of wine or rewarding yourself with a sensual bath. We live in the real world and we know that no matter how much you try to dress it up, an evening with your bank statements is probably not going to be a very thrilling one.

Instead, we'd like to suggest something much more radical, and much more effective: you don't have to try to make money sexy because money already is sexy—more than you would imagine. Just think of the language we use when we talk about money: we talk about having a wad in our pants, pulling in and out of investments, and about cash being hard. Remind you of anything? Money and sex, sex and money: they're intertwined.

We're not talking, of course, about the bottom lines and the rows of numbers, but about the very idea behind money: if you think about it, the main reason we're told not to discuss it with others is because money ties into so many of our insecurities, fears, anxieties, and passions. Some of us, such as Amy, like to kid around and think about the limits of what we would do for cash. Some of us, such as Tony, see a temporary loss of job not merely as a stroke of bad luck, but as an assault on our status as a provider and, therefore, on our worth as a satisfying spouse. And some, such as Eric, find ourselves a bit freaked out when the tables turn and our partner suddenly earns much more than we do.

What we worry about and fret over, of course, is much more than the money itself: into our anxiety about money we fold a thousand other anxieties—about gender roles and sexual prowess and self-worth and personal fulfillment. If we're women, we most likely worry about issues such as stability, safety, and what the future may hold. If we're men, we most likely see any financial setback as reflecting poorly on us in some skewed primitive way, equating loss of income with loss of ability to protect our family. This is why money is so sensitive and why it wreaks so much havoc in relationships.

How, then, should you avoid it? Here's the magical part: you shouldn't. Instead, you should find a way to harness the crazy energy that anxiety about money arouses in all of us and channel it into positive, sexually charged activities. If you're careful enough, you can turn the very same financial force that's bringing you down—this massive and seemingly interminable economic slump— into a sexual force that recharges your relationship. It will not only save it, but it will enhance it considerably.

There are, of course, many ways to do just that and if you've read this book carefully, you know by now that the only solid way to find out what works for you is to think about it and talk about it with your partner. Still, we'd like to offer a few activities that you can try to help release the awesome power of your bank statement into your bedroom. Here goes:

♦ **Role Play**. One of the key difficulties couples have in relationships occurs when for some reason—most likely, a financial catastrophe—the delicate balance that makes things tick is broken and each person finds him or herself in a delicate, painful position. In this current economic downturn, most surveys tell us that this happens more usually than not when men, accustomed to being the primary breadwinners, are laid off and suddenly begin to feel terrified and ashamed, losing their self-respect and their sex drives. To get over such a scenario, we propose a healthy dose of preventive medicine: no matter what your financial situation is, take a night or two every month and practice complete role reversal. If one of you, for example, makes a whole lot more money, that person should, for one evening, pretend to be broke and dependent and let their partner treat them out to a night on the town. This is true even when both partners are more or less equal: having the chance to spend an evening making all of the decisions—or none of them—puts one in an interesting mental position, broadens one's horizons, and makes one more capable of empathizing with others. So go out there and pretend. You can even follow Amy's lead and think about what it might be like to be a prostitute or a gigolo. We are not, of course, advocating you actually do it, but just thinking about it in all its sordid details can be a lot of fun.

♦ **Cash is a Four-Letter Word**. Use it as such. If you understand that the feelings we have about money are about much more than money, why not try to have some fun with it? Take a cue from Megan: from time to time, approach the issue boldly, placing it entirely in a sexual context. You can, for example, ask your recently unemployed spouse who is struggling with mild depression and low self-esteem to quit whining and prove their mettle in bed or tell your overanxious significant other that he or she better start thinking less about interest rates and more about intercourse. Be bold, be brash, be raunchy: the chances are good that you spend most of your time being supportive, kind, and attentive, so there's no reason not to use these very negative feelings and allow yourselves a purely physical, purely pleasurable way to release some steam.

♦ **Condition Yourselves**. Just as the dogs in Pavlov's famous experiment—the ones who got so used to being fed as a bell rang that they started salivating every time they heard the ring, no matter if dinner was served or not—you and your partner have to start conditioning yourselves to think about money as having more to do with the bedroom than with any other room in the house. We know a couple that swore only to have major financial conversation while lying naked in bed: there, fondling one another, they would take on the fake, over-the-top tones so common in erotic movies and talk about investing and saving and diversifying in breathy, sultry voices. Needless to say, pretty soon they were both quite excited about finances and came to see money and everything related to it as something you did in bed—naked and sweating and passionate. Their savings increased 30 percent—and so did their love life.

Again, these are just basic ideas and we hope you can learn to see money—or the lack of it—not as a burden, but as a marital aid, a sexy and enticing instrument to help you thrive. So don't waste any time: take that credit card statement lying on your desk and jump into bed.

The Cost of Breaking Up

If you're going to spend this much on	why not invest instead in
Divorce lawyers: Around $100,000	Cruise around the world: Around $100,000
Separate houses: Around $10,000 a year	Two years' worth of killer vacations: $10,000
Post-breakup dating costs: Around $5,000	A year's worth of weekly soothing couples' massages: Around $5,000
The stress, anger, anxiety, and sadness of breaking up: priceless	The joy, relief, and satisfaction of staying together: priceless

Epilogue

Amy left her office in a hurry. She pushed the elevator button nervously, ran outside the building, and got in her car. She stole a few red lights as she drove, doing her best to keep her speed in check. She knew she couldn't be late.

For the past several months, she and Dan had developed a tradition to help keep their marriage fresh. Realizing that they couldn't afford spending the time or the money required for elaborate, romantic vacations and, refusing to give in to the crushing rhythm of daily life, they decided that each Wednesday, no matter what, they would sneak off at lunchtime, meet downtown, and spend an hour doing something they'd always wanted to do. One week it was trying out a new Japanese restaurant that served strange, raw foods; another it was taking a dance class. The activities were modest—after all, they only had an hour to spend together—but they broke up the day and the week, in an interesting way, giving them something to look forward to.

Finally, Amy arrived at her destination, found a parking spot, and dashed out. A few minutes later, she was strapped inside a kayak, laughing heartily, teasing

Dan about how silly he looked in his oversized orange life vest. They had found out the night before that the city offered free kayak sessions on the river and thought it a perfect summer pastime. Rather than take the kids and turn the whole thing into an exhausting, demanding family outing, they decided kayaking would be their own romantic lunchtime treat. For forty-five minutes, they rowed about, splashing each other gently and enjoying the sun and the air. Then, it was a brief kiss and a happy ride back to the office.

A few days later, having coffee with a friend, Amy described this new tradition of theirs as "relationship ninjutsu." Just like the ancient martial art, she said, she and Dan were using all of the disadvantages of their lives to their own favor. They had little time, little money, and little energy, and so instead of fighting it, they decided to embrace their constraints and find the one loophole that would allow them to be intimate and innovative—even if just for one hour a week. That hour, Amy said, made all the difference in the world.

*   *   *

For Tony and Megan, things weren't quite so peachy. Having finally found a job, Tony now worked endless hours, eager to prove himself to his new employer and quickly climb back up the corporate ladder. When he got home, however, he was too tired to talk—too tired even to be intimate. Megan tried sexy lingerie, cooked lavish dinners, and lit candles, but often experienced with growing frustration her husband pecking her on the cheek and rushing past her to collapse on their bed.

She confronted Tony about her hurt feelings. Feeling guilty, he returned home one night with a pair of costly theater tickets and an invitation to a gala reception, the kind he knew Megan would love. But as she received the gift, tears came to her eyes. She reminded him of the time when he had no money for such luxuries and decided instead to surprise her with an intimate night of reading plays and making love. This, she said, was what she wanted: not expensive gifts, but sweet, heartfelt gestures. If Tony thought that all it took to keep her happy was a hefty expense account, she huffed, he was wrong.

On his end, Tony felt flustered. His time of unemployment and financial anxiety had left its marks on his proud ego and he was eager, now that he was once again doing well for himself, to drown the memory of that terrible time without luxuries. But Megan was telling him that she wanted none of that. What she wanted was him—his time, his attention. And he felt he couldn't give it to her: his new job was just too demanding.

A few tense weeks and a couple of loud fights later, Megan and Tony ended up on the marriage counselor's couch. They both realized there was much work ahead. But sitting there together, holding hands, they agreed to keep communicating their needs and desires and not to revert to old patterns.

*   *   *

Now several months into her new managerial position, Rebecca was beginning to feel the strains of her high-powered job. The excitement over her unlikely promotion quickly wore off and she was left with meetings that ran into the night, business trips to dreary, cold cities, and less and less time to see Eric. Every time she canceled on him, every time she called to say she was too tired to meet, her heart sunk. What if Eric got tired of her and found another woman who didn't work so much and who was around to give him the warmth and care he needed? Rebecca was soon succumbing to anxiety.

To fight it off, she felt like every date she and Eric planned had to be just perfect. She scoffed when he suggested the small, cozy restaurants they used to enjoy and suggested instead fancier, more sophisticated, more expensive places. She surprised him with a romantic weekend getaway to an upscale resort. She bought him a pricey watch she knew he had always wanted. She thought this would make Eric happy, compensate for her absence, and make him know how much she loved him. But Eric was feeling nervous. He wasn't making that much money and couldn't afford to keep up with his girlfriend's costly lifestyle. Yet, with each dinner reservation and fancy gift, he felt the need to reciprocate, to show Rebecca that he, too, cared about her deeply. He thought back to that time, earlier in their relationship, when he spent money uncontrollably to impress Rebecca; he knew he would never allow that to happen again.

One night, over dinner in an elegant French restaurant, Eric suggested a new rule: no date should cost more than $20—split evenly between them. Rebecca agreed, but secretly thought the new idea was impossible. There was not much, she thought, a couple could do for so little money. But the following week, on date night, she realized her mistake. Dressed in his nicest shirt, Eric picked her up at work and instead of hailing a taxi, marched her to the bus stop. They got off near a large supermarket and used most of their limited budget to buy beer, meat, cheese, and delicious bread. Then, they walked to a nearby park, sat down, shared their supplies, and kissed.

They were both giddy. In their new, self-imposed poverty, they transported themselves back in time to the days of their youth when they were broke and hormonal teenagers, with much passion and no cash. Free from the anxieties of restaurant reservations and large bills and rapidly depleting bank accounts, they could focus on what truly mattered—each other.

*   *   *

The three couples depicted in this book may have found their way to happiness, but too many Americans still struggle with the stress of keeping a relationship alive in the face of mounting tensions and growing concerns. With the economy still in the trenches, with many jobs lost and with no obvious solution on the horizon, it is only natural that a lot of our time, energy, and resources be devoted to simply staying afloat.

But as we hope this book has shown—an empty wallet and a dirty mind are truly the only two things you need to save your relationship. If you found the stories in this book inspirational, the advice practical, and the approach helpful—great! But all of that is meaningless without one crucial component: you.

As you put down this book, we hope that you embrace its core message! Remember, just how much small things such as an adult fantasy or a stolen, steamy afternoon with your partner can do for your marriage; that money is just as powerful an aphrodisiac when it's absent as when it's abundant. Your willingness to be proactive, creative, and sexy will keep your relationship in this—or in any other time—alive and flourishing.

We have created a website (www. YouCantAffordToBreakUp.com) where you can find more advice, techniques, and insights about how to keep your relationship rocking. After all, you can't afford to break up.

Bibliography

Becker, Gary S. and Landes, Elizabeth M. and Michael, Robert T. "An Economic Analysis of Marital Instability." *The Journal of Political Economy 85* (Dec.1977): 1141-1187.

Bly, Robert. 1992. *Iron John: A Book about Men.* New York: Vintage.

Boteach, Shmuley. 1999. *Kosher Sex: A Recipe for Passion and Intimacy.* New York: Doubleday.

Bushnell, Candace. 1997. *Sex and the City.* New York: Warner Books.

Buss, David M. 2000. *The Dangerous Passion: Why Jealousy Is As Necessary as Love and Sex.* New York: The Free Press.

Checkhov, Michael. 1993. *On the Technique of Acting. New York :Collins.*

Cole, Toby and Chinoy, Helen. 1949. *Actors on Acting.* New York: Three Rivers Press.

Csikszentmihalyi, Mihaly. 1997. *Finding Flour: The Psychology of Engagement in Everyday Life.* New York: Basic Books.

DeSalvo, Louise. 2000. *Adultery: An Intimate Look at Why People Cheat.* Boston: Beacon Press.

Fitzerald, Mathew. 1999. *Sex-Ploytation: How Women Use Their Bodies to Extort Money from Men.* Willowbrook, Ill.: April House Publishing.

Forsterling, Frederick. 2001. *Attribution East Sussex: Psychology Press, Ltd.*

Gawain, Shakti. 1978. *Creative Visualization.* Mill Valley, CA: Whatever Publishing.

Gelber, Steve. *"Constructing, Repairing and Maintaining Domestic Masculinity." American Quarterly* 49 (1997): 66-112.

Gottman, John M. 1994. *Why Marriages Succeed or Fail… And How You Make Yours Last.* New York: Fireside.

Gray, John M. 1992. *Men Are from Mars, Women Are from Venus.* New York: HarperCollins.

Haley, Jay. 1963. *Strategies of Psychotherapy.* New York: Grune and Stratton.

Haley, Jay. 1978. *Problem Solving Therapy.* New York: Harper and Row.

Hagen, Uta. 1973. *Respect for Acting. New York: Wiley Publishing.*

Hayden, Naura. 1999. *How to Satisfy a Woman Every Time…And Have Her Beg for More. New York: St. Martin's Press.*

Heys, Dalma. 1977. Erotic Silence of the American Wife. New York: Plume.

Hite, Shere. 1976. *The Hite Report: A Nationwide Study of Female Sexuality.* New York: Macmillan.

Hite, Shere. 1981. *The Hite Report on Male Sexuality.* New York: Knopf.

Horan, Nancy. 2008. *Loving Frank.* New York: Ballantine Books.

Jong, Erica. 1973. *Fear of Flying.* New York: Holt, Rinehart and Winston.

Klein, Melanie. 1975. *The Psycho-Analysis of Children in Collected Works.* London: Hagarth.

Landy, Eugene. 1971. *The Underground Dictionary.* New York: Simon and Schuster.

Leach, Michael, and Theresa J. Borchard (Editors). 2002. *I Like Being Married: Treasured Traditions, Ritual and Stories.* New York: Pantheon Books.

Levy, Howard S. and Ishihara, Akira. 1970. *The Tao of Sex.* New York: Harper and Row.

Morrin, Jack. 1995. *The Erotic Mind: Unlocking the Inner Sources of Sexual Passion and Fulfillment.* New York: HarperCollins.

Phillips, Adam. 1997. *Monogamy.* New York: Pantheon.

Raiti, Gerard C. "Mobile Intimacy Theories on the Economics of Emotion with Examples from Asia." Journal of Media Culture 10.1, 2007: 1-10.

Stanislavski, Constantin. 1948. *My Life in Art.* New York: Theatre Arts Book.

Stanislavski, Constantin. 1963. *An Actor's Handbook.* New York: Theatre Arts Book.

Stanislavski, Constantin. 1989. *Building a Character.* New York: Theatre Arts Book.

Stanislavski, Constantin. 1989. *An Actor Prepares.* New York: Theatre Arts Book.

Stanfield, James R. and Stanfield, Jaqueline B. *Where has love gone? Reciprocity, Redistribution and Nurturance Gap.* Journal of Socio-Economics 26, 1997: 111-126.

Staheli, Lana. 1977. *Triangles: Understanding, Preventing and Surviving an Affair.* New York: HarperCollins.

Talese, Gay. 1980. *Thy Neighbor's Wife.* Garden City, New York: Doubleday.

Twitchell, James B. 2006. *Why Men Hide.* New York: Columbia University Press.

Winnicott, D.W. 1988. *Human Nature.* New York: Schocken Books.